Personal tax

(Finance Act 2014)

Workbook

For assessments from January 2015

Aubrey Penning

Bob Thomas

Published by Osborne Books Limited
Unit 1B Everoak Estate
Bromyard Road, Worcester WR2 5HP
Tel 01905 748071
Email books@osbornebooks.co.uk
Website www.osbornebooks.co.uk

Design by Laura Ingham

Printed by CPI Group (UK) Limited, Croydon, CRO 4YY, on environmentally friendly, acid-free paper from managed forests.

British Library Cataloguing in Publication Data
A catalogue record for this book is available from the British Library

ISBN 978 1909173 507

Contents

Acknowledgements

The publisher wishes to thank the following for their help with the reading and production of the book: Jon Moore, Bee Pugh and Cathy Turner. Thanks are also due to Laura Ingham for her designs for this series.

The publisher is indebted to the Association of Accounting Technicians for its help and advice to our author and editor during the preparation of this text.

Author and Technical Editor

Aubrey Penning has many years experience of teaching accountancy on a variety of courses in Worcester and Gwent. He is a Certified Accountant, and before his move into full-time teaching he worked for the health service, a housing association and a chemical supplier. For many years he was the AAT course coordinator at Worcester College of Technology, specialising in the areas of management accounting and taxation.

Bob Thomas, the Technical Editor of this book, has been involved with the Education and Training activities of the AAT since 1986, including the development and piloting of the skills-based scheme. He is an external verifier, a simulation writer, a moderator and a contributor at workshops, training days, conferences and master classes. Until recently he was a member of the Learning and Development Board and Chairman of the Assessment Panel.

Introduction

what this book covers

This book has been written to cover the 'Personal tax' Unit which is an optional Unit for the revised (2013) AAT Level 4 Diploma in Accounting.

what this book contains

This book is set out in two sections:

■ **Chapter Activities** which provide extra practice material in addition to the activities included in the Osborne Books Tutorial text. Answers to the Chapter activities are included in this book.

■ **Practice Assessments** are provided to prepare the student for the Computer Based Assessments. They are based directly on the structure, style and content of the sample assessment material provided by the AAT at www.aat.org.uk. Suggested answers to the Practice Assessments are set out in this book.

further information

If you want to know more about our products and resources, please visit www.osbornebooks.co.uk for further details and access to our online shop.

Chapter activities

1   Introduction to income tax

1.1   State whether each of the following statements is true or false.

✔

		True	False
(a)	An individual's tax records only need to be kept until one year after the end of the tax year, unless an investigation is being carried out		
(b)	It is not the taxpayer's responsibility to inform HMRC of any untaxed taxable income, unless they have been asked to complete a tax return		
(c)	Accountants must normally follow the rules of confidentiality, but there are exceptions		
(d)	Where a practitioner has knowledge or suspicion that his client is money laundering, then he has a duty to inform the relevant person or authority		
(e)	Accountants should warn clients if they suspect money laundering to give the client a chance to cease the activity		
(f)	When an accountant is advising a client the greatest duty of care is to the client		

1.2   State which of the following can provide sources of information about tax law and its interpretation.

✔

		Yes	No
(a)	HMRC extra-statutory concessions		
(b)	Statute law		
(c)	HMRC statements of practice		
(d)	Case law		
(e)	Website www.hmrc.gov.uk		
(f)	Website www.statistics.gov.uk		
(g)	HMRC guides and help sheets		

1.3 Match the following examples of income with the correct income category.

Sample Income	Income Category
UK dividends	Property Income
Partnership profits	Savings and Investment Income
Rents from land	Trading Income
Earnings from a job	Employment, Pension and Social Security Income

1.4 Tick the columns to show which of the following categories of income is taxed on an accruals basis, and which is on a receipts basis (ie based on when received).

✔

Income Category	Accruals Basis	Receipts Basis
Property Income		
Savings and Investment Income		
Trading Income		
Employment, Pension and Social Security Income		

1.5 State which of the following types of income are exempt from income tax.

✔

Income Category	Exempt	Not Exempt
(a) Employment income		
(b) Income from a NISA		
(c) Premium bond prizes		
(d) Rent received from a buy-to-let property		
(e) Betting winnings (unless a professional gambler)		
(f) Lottery prizes		

2 Income from property

2.1 Chester has two properties in addition to his home, details of which are as follows:

Two bedroom house:

(1) This unfurnished house is rented out for £850 per month. The property was occupied this tax year until 1 February when the tenants suddenly moved out, owing the rent for January. Chester knows that he will not recover this rent. The property was let again from 1 May to another family.

(2) Chester had to pay £530 for redecoration in March following the poor condition of the property at that time.

(3) The only other expense paid by Chester on the house was 10% management charge to the agent on rent received.

One bedroom flat:

(1) This furnished flat is rented out for £550 per month. The property was rented all tax year.

(2) Chester paid council tax and water rates on the flat, totalling £1,100 for the period that the flat was occupied. He also paid buildings and contents insurance of £340 for the year.

Calculate the profit or loss made on each property, using the following table.

	Two bedroom house £	One bedroom flat £
Income		
Expenses:		

2.2   Select the statements that are true from the following: ✔

		True	False
(a)	The maximum amount of gross rent that can be received tax free under the rent a room scheme is £5,250		
(b)	The rent a room scheme only applies to furnished accommodation		
(c)	Rent a room relief can be claimed for guest houses provided it is also the claimant's main residence		
(d)	Taxpayers can claim both rent a room relief and wear and tear allowance for the same property		
(e)	Eligible taxpayers do not have to claim rent a room relief if they choose not to		
(f)	Rent a room relief can only be claimed by owner-occupiers		
(g)	Charges for goods or services like food or laundry are ignored when calculating the gross rent		

2.3   Sienna owns a field where she has three static caravans that are rented out to holidaymakers. The caravans are available to the public for rent from 1 March to 31 October each year. This year, during this period there were three weeks when the caravans were unoccupied. Sienna carries out the caravan rentals on a commercial basis.

Select the statements that are true from the following:

✔

		True	False
(a)	The rental of caravans qualifies as furnished holiday lettings		
(b)	The rental of caravans is treated as a hobby and is exempt from tax		
(c)	Although the caravans are furnished, wear and tear allowance cannot be claimed as these are holiday lettings		
(d)	Interest on loans to buy the caravans can be claimed as allowable expenses		
(e)	Rent a room relief can be claimed against the rental income		

2.4   Mahjabeen rents a furnished room in his own house to a lodger for £210 per week, including an evening meal. Heating the room costs Mahjabeen £150 for the year, and food for the lodger's meals costs £15 per week.

(a)   Calculate the assessable amount for the tax year, based on

(1)   claiming rent a room relief, and

(2)   preparing a normal rental income computation

using the following table.

	Claiming rent a room relief £	Normal rental income computation £
Income	10,920	10,920
Allowable deductions		

(b)   Complete the following sentence:

To pay the minimum income tax, Mahjabeen should **claim / not claim** rent a room relief.

2.5 Stephan rents out one furnished property. He claims wear and tear allowance. The following is a statement compiled from his accounting records relating to the tax year.

	£	£
Rental Income Receivable		12,000
less expenditure:		
Council Tax	700	
Water Rates	300	
Insurance	380	
Cost of replacement furniture	2,100	
Depreciation of furniture	800	
Managing Agent's Charges	1,200	
		5,480
Profit		6,520

Required:

(a) Calculate the assessable property income for Stephan, using the following table.

	£	£
Income		
Expenditure:		
Assessable Income		

(b) Complete page UKP2 of the UK Property supplementary pages, (2013/14 version reproduced on the next page) for Stephan.

Property income

Do not include furnished holiday lettings, Real Estate Investment Trust or Property Authorised Investment Funds dividends/distributions here.

20 Total rents and other income from property

£ [   ] . [0] [0]

21 Tax taken off any income in box 20 - *read the notes*

£ [   ] . [0] [0]

22 Premiums for the grant of a lease - from box E on the Working Sheet - *read the notes*

£ [   ] . [0] [0]

23 Reverse premiums and inducements

£ [   ] . [0] [0]

Property expenses

24 Rent, rates, insurance, ground rents etc.

£ [   ] . [0] [0]

25 Property repairs and maintenance

£ [   ] . [0] [0]

26 Loan interest and other financial costs

£ [   ] . [0] [0]

27 Legal, management and other professional fees

£ [   ] . [0] [0]

28 Costs of services provided, including wages

£ [   ] . [0] [0]

29 Other allowable property expenses

£ [   ] . [0] [0]

Calculating your taxable profit or loss

30 Private use adjustment - *read the notes*

£ [   ] . [0] [0]

31 Balancing charges - *read the notes*

£ [   ] . [0] [0]

32 Annual Investment Allowance

£ [   ] . [0] [0]

33 Business Premises Renovation Allowance (Assisted Areas only) - *read the notes*

£ [   ] . [0] [0]

34 All other capital allowances

£ [   ] . [0] [0]

35 Landlord's Energy Saving Allowance

£ [   ] . [0] [0]

36 10% wear and tear allowance - *for furnished residential accommodation only*

£ [   ] . [0] [0]

37 Rent a Room exempt amount

£ [   ] . [0] [0]

38 Adjusted profit for the year - from box O on the Working Sheet - *read the notes*

£ [   ] . [0] [0]

39 Loss brought forward used against this year's profits

£ [   ] . [0] [0]

40 Taxable profit for the year (box 38 minus box 39)

£ [   ] . [0] [0]

41 Adjusted loss for the year - from box O on the Working Sheet - *read the notes*

£ [   ] . [0] [0]

42 Loss set off against 2013-14 total income - *this will be unusual - read the notes*

£ [   ] . [0] [0]

43 Loss to carry forward to following year, including unused losses brought forward

£ [   ] . [0] [0]

3 Income from savings and investments

3.1 Some taxable interest is received gross, and some is received net of 20% tax. Examine the following list of income sources, and analyse it into the way that interest is received, using the table.

- Loan stock from quoted company
- Local authority loan
- Treasury stock (a type of Gilt)
- Online building society account

Received net	Received gross

3.2 During the tax year, Wesley received UK dividends of £900 and £480 interest from his building society account.

(a) What is the total amount of tax that is treated as already paid?

✔

(a)	None	
(b)	£345	
(c)	£220	
(d)	£100	

(b) What is the total assessable income from these sources for the tax year?

✔

(a)	£1,380	
(b)	£1,480	
(c)	£1,725	
(d)	£1,600	

3.3 State which of the following sources provide tax-free (exempt) income:

	✔
(a) Government Stocks (Gilts)	
(b) UK Dividends	
(c) Building Society Cash ISA	
(d) Bank ISA operated by post	
(e) Local Authority Loans	

3.4 Complete the following table to show the maximum investment in a NISA that an individual can make from July 2014, in 2014/15 tax year.

Total NISA limit	

3.5 Katherine has received the amounts shown on the following table from various investments. Complete the table to show the assessable amounts and the amounts of tax that are treated as having been paid.

Investment	Amount Received £	Assessable Amount £	Tax treated as paid £
Bank Account	560		
UK Dividends	2,700		
Cash NISA	120		
Debenture interest	800		
Totals	4,180		

4 Income from employment

4.1 Complete the following table by correctly matching the indicators as relating to employment or self-employment.

Indicators of Employment	Indicators of Self Employment

Indicators

- Choose work hours and invoice for work done
- Need to do the work yourself
- Told how, where and when to do work
- No risk of capital or losses
- Work for several people or organisations
- Decide yourself how, when and where to do work
- Can employ helper or substitute
- Employer provides equipment
- Risk own capital and bear losses from work that is not to standard
- Work set hours and paid regular wage with sick pay and holidays
- Usually work for one employer
- Provide own equipment

4.2 **(a)** What scale charge percentage would be applied for petrol cars with the following CO_2 emissions?

    (1)   111 g/km

    (2)   134 g/km

    (3)   151 g/km

    (4)   249 g/km

(b) Silvia was provided with a second hand car on 6 October 2014. It cost the company £8,000, but the list price of this car when bought new was £17,000. The car has a CO_2 emission of 168g/km, and has a diesel engine. The company pays for all running costs, except private fuel.

    (1)   The cost of the car used in the benefit in kind computation is

    £ _____

    (2)   The percentage used in the benefit in kind computation is

    _____ %

    (3)   The assessable benefit for Silvia relating to the car for 2014/15 is

    £ _____

4.3 **(a)** When accommodation is purchased by an employer, what is the value of the property above which an additional benefit is applied?

		✔
(a)	£60,000	
(b)	£70,000	
(c)	£75,000	
(d)	£80,000	
(e)	£100,000	
(f)	£125,000	

(b) Would the following situations be treated as being job-related where no accommodation benefit arises?

		Yes	No
(a)	House provided for a vicar		
(b)	House provided by employer for accountant working for a housing association		
(c)	Flat in sheltered accommodation provided for an on-site care manager		

(c)   Summer was provided with accommodation in the form of a flat that the employer purchased for £165,000. It is not job related. The flat has an annual value £9,300. Summer pays £200 per month towards the private use of the flat. Assume that the HMRC official interest rate is 3.25%. Her taxable benefit is:

✔

(a)	£6,900	
(b)	£9,300	
(c)	£9,825	
(d)	£14,662	

4.4   On 6 December 2014, Kevin was provided with a company loan of £16,000 on which he pays interest at 1.5% per annum. On 6 February 2015 Kevin repaid £2,000. The official rate of interest is 3.25%.

What is the benefit in kind for 2014/15 to the nearest £?

4.5 **(a)** Dee uses her own car for business travelling. During the tax year she travelled 11,500 business miles for which she was paid 50p per mile by her employer. The impact of this is:

		✔
(a)	She will have a taxable amount of £575	
(b)	She will have a taxable amount of £875	
(c)	She will claim an allowable expense of £875	
(d)	She will claim an allowable expense of £575	

(b) Eddie has an occupational pension scheme to which he contributes 5% of his salary. His employer contributes 6% of his salary. His salary was £28,400. The impact of this is:

		✔
(a)	His taxable salary will be increased by £1,704	
(b)	His taxable salary will be reduced by £1,420	
(c)	His taxable salary will be increased by £284	
(d)	His basic rate band will be extended by £1,775	

(c) Steve pays £300 per year in subscriptions to professional bodies. His employer reimburses him £180. The overall impact of this is:

		✔
(a)	No impact on tax	
(b)	An allowable deduction of £120	
(c)	A benefit of £180	
(d)	An allowable deduction of £300	

(d) Genna has a non-contributory occupational pension scheme. This means:

		✔
(a)	The employer pays a percentage of her salary into the scheme, but Genna does not	
(b)	Genna pays a percentage of her salary into the scheme, but the employer does not	
(c)	Only the Government pays a percentage of her salary into the scheme	
(d)	Genna and the Government both pay a percentage of her salary into the scheme	

5   Preparing income tax computations

5.1   Richard, who was born in 1935, had pension income of £27,000 and received dividends of £1,215.

He paid £400 (net) to charities under the gift aid scheme.

Calculate his total income tax liability (ie before deduction of tax paid) for the tax year, using the table given below.

	£
Pension Income	
Gross dividends	
Personal allowance	
Taxable income	

5.2 Select from the following statements, those which are correct.

		True	False
(a)	Payments on account relating to a tax year are paid on 31 January in the tax year, and on 31 July following the tax year		
(b)	The final payment of income tax relating to a tax year is paid on 31 October following the end of the tax year		
(c)	If a taxpayer is late paying income tax then he will either be subject to a penalty or interest, but not both		
(d)	If a tax return is submitted on 31 March following the end of the tax year, the taxpayer would be subject to a penalty of £150		
(e)	If a tax return is submitted on 31 May (approximately 14 months after the end of the tax year), the taxpayer would be subject to a penalty of £100 plus a daily penalty		
(f)	Late payment of a final balancing payment of income tax by more than 30 days will be subject to a penalty of 5% of the tax due		

5.3 Charlie is a higher rate taxpayer. He deliberately concealed the dividends that he received when he completed his tax return.

Select the correct statement from the following.

		True	False
(a)	Charlie did nothing wrong as the tax on dividends has already been deducted		
(b)	Charlie did nothing wrong as dividends are exempt from income tax		
(c)	Charlie will be subject to a penalty of between 30% and 100% of the dividend income that he has not declared		
(d)	Charlie will be subject to a penalty of between 30% and 100% of the extra income tax that is due on the dividends		
(e)	Charlie cannot be charged a penalty if it is his first offence		

5.4   Wayne earns £45,000 per year from his job as a sales manager, and is entitled to a diesel company car and all fuel (business and private). The car has a list price of £22,000, but was purchased at a discount for £19,500. It has emissions of 159 g/km.

Wayne makes cash contributions of £1,600 per year into a personal pension scheme.

Calculate Wayne's tax liability (to the nearest £), using the following table.

Workings	
	£
Salary	
Car benefit	
Fuel Benefit	
Personal allowance	
Taxable income	
Tax at 20%:	
Tax at 40%:	
Total tax liability	

5.5 Mike earns £45,000 per year from his job, and is entitled to a petrol company car and all fuel (business and private). The car has a list price of £16,000. It has emissions of 129 g/km.

Mike also received an interest free loan from his employer of £12,000 on 6 October in the tax year. He has not made any repayments.

Mike paid his own professional subscriptions of £200.

Assume that the official HMRC rate is 3.25%.

Complete supplementary page E1 of Mike's tax return as far as possible (see next page for the 2013/14 version).

5.6 Rachel had employment income of £91,500 and received dividends of £15,750. She paid £1,200 (net) into a personal pension scheme.

Calculate her total income tax liability (ie before deduction of tax paid) for the tax year, using the table given below.

	£
Employment Income	
Gross dividends	
Personal allowance	
Taxable income	

5.5 continued...

![HM Revenue & Customs logo] **HM Revenue & Customs**

Employment
Tax year 6 April 2013 to 5 April 2014

Your name

Your Unique Taxpayer Reference (UTR)

Complete an *Employment* page for each employment or directorship

1 Pay from this employment – the total from your P45 or P60 - *before tax was taken off*

£ · 0 0

2 UK tax taken off pay in box 1

£ · 0 0

3 Tips and other payments not on your P60 - *read the Employment notes*

£ · 0 0

4 PAYE tax reference of your employer (on your P45/P60)

/

5 Your employer's name

6 If you were a company director, put 'X' in the box

7 And, if the company was a close company, put 'X' in the box

8 If you are a part-time teacher in England or Wales and are on the Repayment of Teachers' Loans Scheme for this employment, put 'X' in the box

Benefits from your employment - use your form P11D (or equivalent information)

9 Company cars and vans - *the total 'cash equivalent' amount*

£ · 0 0

10 Fuel for company cars and vans - *the total 'cash equivalent' amount*

£ · 0 0

11 Private medical and dental insurance - *the total 'cash equivalent' amount*

£ · 0 0

12 Vouchers, credit cards and excess mileage allowance

£ · 0 0

13 Goods and other assets provided by your employer - *the total value or amount*

£ · 0 0

14 Accommodation provided by your employer - *the total value or amount*

£ · 0 0

15 Other benefits (including interest-free and low interest loans) - *the total 'cash equivalent' amount*

£ · 0 0

16 Expenses payments received and balancing charges

£ · 0 0

Employment expenses

17 Business travel and subsistence expenses

£ · 0 0

18 Fixed deductions for expenses

£ · 0 0

19 Professional fees and subscriptions

£ · 0 0

20 Other expenses and capital allowances

£ · 0 0

ℹ **Share schemes, employment lump sums, compensation, deductions and Seafarers' Earnings Deduction** are on the *Additional information* pages enclosed in the tax return pack.

SA102 2014   Page E 1   HMRC 12/13

6   Capital gains tax – the main principles

6.1   For each statement, tick the appropriate box.

		Actual Proceeds Used	Deemed proceeds used	No gain or loss basis
(a)	Father gives an asset to his son			
(b)	Wife sells an asset to her husband			
(c)	Simon gives an asset to his friend			
(d)	Margaret sells an asset to her cousin for £15,000 when the market value is £40,000			
(e)	Brian gives an asset to his civil partner, Dave			

6.2   Alex bought an asset in January 2008 for £36,000, selling it in December 2014 for £35,000. He paid auctioneers commission of 4% when he bought the asset and 5% when he sold the asset.

The loss on this asset is:

(a)	£nil	
(b)	£1,000	
(c)	£4,190	
(d)	£2,440	

True or false: legal fees are an allowable deduction where they relate to the purchase or sale of an asset.

6.3   State which of the following statements are true:

	True	False
(a) The annual exemption is applied after capital losses are deducted		
(b) Capital losses from the same year cannot safeguard the annual exemption		
(c) Capital gains are taxed at 28% for higher rate tax payers		
(d) Capital losses can be set against gains of the previous tax year		
(e) Capital losses brought forward can safeguard the annual exemption when offset against current year gains		

6.4   Josie has a capital loss brought forward of £4,000. She is a higher rate income tax payer.

She sold an asset during the tax year for £19,000. She had been given the asset by her husband when it was worth £8,000. Her husband originally paid £6,500 for the asset.

Complete the following sentences:

(a)   The gain on the asset is   £

(b)   The amount of loss that will be relieved is   £

(c)   The capital gains tax payable is   £

(d)   The loss to be carried forward to the next tax year is   £

6.5   Complete the following table to show which assets are exempt from capital gains tax and which are chargeable.

Asset	Exempt	Chargeable
Antique furniture valued at £30,000		
Principal private residence		
Clock		
Shares		
Holiday home		
Government securities		
Vintage car		
Land		

7   Capital gains tax – some special rules

7.1   Richard bought a house on 1 January 2000 for £125,000. He lived in the house until 31 December 2002 when he moved abroad for one year to work. He returned from abroad on 31 December 2003, and then immediately moved into his elderly father's house until 30 June 2005, leaving his own home empty. He then moved back into his own house until 31 December 2011, when he moved to a new home and put the house on the market. The house was eventually sold on 1 January 2015 for £205,000.

(a)   Which periods are treated as occupied and which are not?

Occupation / Deemed Occupation	Non-occupation

(b)   What is the chargeable gain on the property?

£

7.2 The following table relates to sales of chattels.

Match the statements shown below to the correct asset details.

Asset	Sale proceeds	Cost	Statement
1	£4,000	£7,000	
2	£14,000	£8,000	
3	£8,000	£3,000	
4	£3,000	£5,000	
5	£15,000	£21,000	

Statements:
- Exempt asset
- Calculate gain as normal
- Calculate loss as normal
- Sale proceeds to be £6,000
- Chattel marginal relief applies

7.3 Paul bought 20,000 shares in Lincoln Ltd for £5 per share in October 2000. He received a bonus issue of 1 for 25 shares in March 2003. In January 2015, Paul sold 8,000 shares for £9 per share.

Clearly showing the balance of shares, and their value, to carry forward, calculate the gain made on these shares. All workings must be shown in your calculations.

7.4   Bob sold the following assets in August 2014. These were his only disposals during the tax year.

Description	Sale Proceeds £	Cost £
Holiday home	230,000	150,000
Listed shares in B plc	20,000	35,000
Listed shares in C plc	18,000	10,000
Unlisted shares in D ltd	48,000	32,000

Use this information to complete pages CG1 and CG2 of Bob's tax return.

The 2013/14 version is shown on the next pages.

HM Revenue & Customs

Capital gains summary
Tax year 6 April 2013 to 5 April 2014

1	Your name

2	Your Unique Taxpayer Reference (UTR)

Summary of your enclosed computations

Please read the *Capital gains summary notes* before filling in this section. **You must enclose your computations, including details of each gain or loss, as well as filling in the boxes.**

ℹ️ To get notes and helpsheets that will help you fill in this form, go to hmrc.gov.uk/selfassessmentforms

3 Total gains *(Boxes 21 + 27 + 33 + 34)*
£ · 0 0

4 Gains qualifying for Entrepreneurs' Relief (but excluding gains deferred from before 23 June 2010) - *read the notes*
£ · 0 0

5 Gains invested under Seed Enterprise Investment Scheme and qualifying for exemption - *read the notes*
£ · 0 0

6 Total losses of the year - *enter '0' if there are none*
£ · 0 0

7 Losses brought forward and used in the year
£ · 0 0

8 Adjustment to Capital Gains Tax - *read the notes*
£ · 0 0

9 Additional liability for non-resident or dual resident trusts
£ · 0 0

10 Losses available to be carried forward to later years
£ · 0 0

11 Losses used against an earlier year's gain (special circumstances apply - *read the notes*)
£ · 0 0

12 Losses used against income – amount claimed against 2013–14 income - *read the notes*
£ · 0 0

13 Amount in box 12 relating to shares to which Enterprise Investment Scheme/Seed Enterprise Investment Scheme relief is attributable
£ · 0 0

14 Losses used against income – amount claimed against 2012–13 income - *read the notes*
£ · 0 0

15 Amount in box 14 relating to shares to which Enterprise Investment Scheme/Seed Enterprise Investment Scheme relief is attributable
£ · 0 0

16 Income losses of 2013–14 set against gains
£ · 0 0

17 Deferred gains from before 23 June 2010 qualifying for Entrepreneurs' Relief
£ · 0 0

Listed shares and securities

| 18 | Number of disposals - *read the notes* |
| 21 | Gains in the year, before losses |
£ · 0 0

| 19 | Disposal proceeds |
£ · 0 0

| 22 | If you are making any claim or election, put 'X' in the box |

| 20 | Allowable costs (including purchase price) |
£ · 0 0

| 23 | If your computations include any estimates or valuations, put 'X' in the box |

Unlisted shares and securities

| 24 | Number of disposals - *read the notes* |

| 27 | Gains in the year, before losses |
£ · 0 0

| 25 | Disposal proceeds |
£ · 0 0

| 28 | If you are making any claim or election, put 'X' in the box |

| 26 | Allowable costs (including purchase price) |
£ · 0 0

| 29 | If your computations include any estimates or valuations, put 'X' in the box |

Property and other assets and gains

| 30 | Number of disposals |

| 34 | Attributed gains where personal losses cannot be set off |
£ · 0 0

| 31 | Disposal proceeds |
£ · 0 0

| 35 | If you are making any claim or election, put 'X' in the box |

| 32 | Allowable costs (including purchase price) |
£ · 0 0

| 36 | If your computations include any estimates or valuations, put 'X' in the box |

| 33 | Gains in the year, before losses |
£ · 0 0

Any other information

| 37 | Please give any other information in this space |

7.5   Jason disposed of three assets during the tax year as follows:

- An antique painting was sold for £12,100. It had been bought for £3,000.

- A quarter acre piece of land was sold for £10,000. It had been bought as part of a two-acre plot for £12,000. The remaining land was valued at £15,000 at the time of the sale.

- A holiday cottage was sold for £230,000. It had been bought for £195,000, and Jason had spent £38,000 extending it.

Jason is a higher rate income tax payer.

Complete the following sentences:

(a)   The gain on the painting is

£

(b)   The gain on the land is

£

(c)   The result of the sale of the holiday cottage is a gain / loss of

£

(d)   The capital gains tax payable is

£

Chapter activities
answers

1 Introduction to income tax

1.1

		True	False
(a)	An individual's tax records only need to be kept until one year after the end of the tax year, unless an investigation is being carried out		✔
(b)	It is not the taxpayer's responsibility to inform HMRC of any untaxed taxable income, unless they have been asked to complete a tax return		✔
(c)	Accountants must normally follow the rules of confidentiality, but there are exceptions	✔	
(d)	Where a practitioner has knowledge or suspicion that his client is money laundering, then he has a duty to inform the relevant person or authority	✔	
(e)	Accountants should warn clients if they suspect money laundering to give the client a chance to cease the activity		✔
(f)	When an accountant is advising a client the greatest duty of care is to the client	✔	

1.2

		Yes	No
(a)	HMRC extra-statutory concessions	✔	
(b)	Statute law	✔	
(c)	HMRC statements of practice	✔	
(d)	Case law	✔	
(e)	Website www.hmrc.gov.uk	✔	
(f)	Website www.statistics.gov.uk		✔
(g)	HMRC guides and help sheets	✔	

1.3

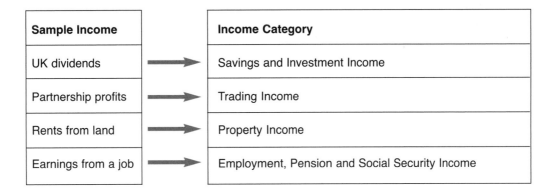

Sample Income		Income Category
UK dividends	→	Savings and Investment Income
Partnership profits	→	Trading Income
Rents from land	→	Property Income
Earnings from a job	→	Employment, Pension and Social Security Income

1.4

Income Category	Accruals Basis	Receipts Basis
Property Income	✔	
Savings and Investment Income		✔
Trading Income	✔	
Employment, Pension and Social Security Income		✔

1.5

Income Category	Exempt	Not Exempt
(a) Employment income		✔
(b) Income from a NISA	✔	
(c) Premium bond prizes	✔	
(d) Rent received from a buy-to-let property		✔
(e) Betting winnings (unless a professional gambler)	✔	
(f) Lottery prizes	✔	

2 Income from property

2.1

	Two bedroom house	One bedroom flat
	£	£
Income	8,500	6,600
Expenses:		
Irrecoverable rent	850	
Management fees	765	
Redecoration	530	
Council Tax & Water		1,100
Insurance		340
Wear & Tear Allowance		550
Profit	6,355	4,610

2.2

	True	False
(a) The maximum amount of gross rent that can be received tax free under the rent a room scheme is £5,250.		✔
(b) The rent a room scheme only applies to furnished accommodation.	✔	
(c) Rent a room relief can be claimed for guest houses provided it is also the claimant's main residence.	✔	
(d) Taxpayers can claim both rent a room relief and wear and tear allowance for the same property.		✔
(e) Eligible taxpayers do not have to claim rent a room relief if they choose not to.	✔	
(f) Rent a room relief can only be claimed by owner-occupiers.		✔
(g) Charges for goods or services like food or laundry are ignored when calculating the gross rent.		✔

2.3

		True	False
(a)	The rental of caravans qualifies as furnished holiday lettings	✔	
(b)	The rental of caravans is treated as a hobby and is exempt from tax		✔
(c)	Although the caravans are furnished, wear and tear allowance cannot be claimed as these are holiday lettings	✔	
(d)	Interest on loans to buy the caravans can be claimed as allowable expenses	✔	
(e)	Rent a room relief can be claimed against the rental income		✔

2.4 **(a)**

	Claiming rent a room relief	Normal rental income computation
	£	£
Income	10,920	10,920
Allowable deductions:		
Rent a room relief	4,250	
Heating		150
Food		780
Wear and Tear Allowance		1,092
Assessable amount	6,670	8,898

(b) To pay the minimum income tax, Mahjabeen should **claim** rent a room relief.

2.5 **(a)**

	£	£
Income		12,000
Expenditure:		
Council tax	700	
Water rates	300	
Insurance	380	
Managing agent's charges	1,200	
Wear and tear (10% x [12,000 – 700 – 300])	1,100	
		3,680
Assessable Income		8,320

(b) Property income

Do not include furnished holiday lettings, Real Estate Investment Trust or Property Authorised Investment Funds dividends/distributions here.

20	Total rents and other income from property	22	Premiums for the grant of a lease – from box E on the Working Sheet – *read the notes*
	£ 1 2 0 0 0 · 0 0		£ · 0 0

21	Tax taken off any income in box 20 – *read the notes*	23	Reverse premiums and inducements
	£ · 0 0		£ · 0 0

Property expenses

24	Rent, rates, insurance, ground rents etc.	27	Legal, management and other professional fees
	£ 1 3 8 0 · 0 0		£ 1 2 0 0 · 0 0

25	Property repairs and maintenance	28	Costs of services provided, including wages
	£ · 0 0		£ · 0 0

26	Loan interest and other financial costs	29	Other allowable property expenses
	£ · 0 0		£ · 0 0

Calculating your taxable profit or loss

30	Private use adjustment – *read the notes*	37	Rent a Room exempt amount
	£ · 0 0		£ · 0 0

31	Balancing charges – *read the notes*	38	Adjusted profit for the year – from box O on the Working Sheet – *read the notes*
	£ · 0 0		£ 8 3 2 0 · 0 0

32	Annual Investment Allowance	39	Loss brought forward used against this year's profits
	£ · 0 0		£ · 0 0

33	Business Premises Renovation Allowance (Assisted Areas only) – *read the notes*	40	Taxable profit for the year (box 38 minus box 39)
	£ · 0 0		£ 8 3 2 0 · 0 0

34	All other capital allowances	41	Adjusted loss for the year – from box O on the Working Sheet – *read the notes*
	£ · 0 0		£ · 0 0

35	Landlord's Energy Saving Allowance	42	Loss set off against 2013–14 total income – *this will be unusual – read the notes*
	£ · 0 0		£ · 0 0

36	10% wear and tear allowance – *for furnished residential accommodation only*	43	Loss to carry forward to following year, including unused losses brought forward
	£ 1 1 0 0 · 0 0		£ · 0 0

3 Income from savings and investments

3.1

Received net	Received gross
Loan stock from quoted company	Treasury stock (a type of Gilt)
Local authority loan	
Online building society account	

3.2 **(a)** (c) £220 (tax credit on dividends of £900 x 10/90 plus tax on building society account of £480 x 20/80 is treated as tax already paid)

(b) (d) £1,600 (dividends plus tax credit £1,000 + gross interest £600)

3.3

(a) Government Stocks (Gilts)	
(b) UK Dividends	
(c) Building Society Cash ISA	✔
(d) Bank ISA operated by post	✔
(e) Local Authority Loans	

3.4

Total NISA limit	£15,000

3.5

Investment	Amount Received £	Assessable Amount £	Tax treated as paid £
Bank Account	560	700	140
UK Dividends	2,700	3,000	300
Cash NISA	120	0	0
Debenture interest	800	1,000	200
Totals	4,180	4,700	640

4 Income from employment

4.1

Indicators of Employment	Indicators of Self Employment
Need to do the work yourself	Can employ helper or substitute
Told how, where and when to do work	Decide yourself how, when and where to do work
Work set hours and paid regular wage with sick pay and holidays	Choose work hours and invoice for work done
No risk of capital or losses	Risk own capital and bear losses from work that is not to standard
Employer provides equipment	Provide own equipment
Usually work for one employer	Work for several people or organisations

4.2 **(a)**

    (1)   111 g/km   15%

    (2)   134 g/km   19%

    (3)   151 g/km   23%

    (4)   249 g/km   35%

  (b)

    (1)   The cost of the car used in the benefit in kind computation is **£17,000**

    (2)   The percentage used in the benefit in kind computation is **29%**

    (3)   The assessable benefit for Silvia relating to the car for 2014/15 is **£2,465**

4.3 **(a)**   £75,000

  (b)

		Yes	No
(a)	House provided for a vicar	✔	
(b)	House provided by employer for accountant working for a housing association		✔
(c)	Flat in sheltered accommodation provided for an on-site care manager	✔	

  (c)   £9,825   *(£9,300 + (3.25% x £90,000) – £2,400)*

4.4 £87 *(£16,000 + £14,000)/2 x 4/12 x (3.25% – 1.5%)*

4.5 **(a)** (b) She will have a taxable amount of £875

(10,000 x (50p – 45p)) + (1,500 x (50p – 25p))

(b) (b) His taxable salary will be reduced by £1,420

(£28,400 x 5%, the employer's contribution is tax-free)

(c) (b) An allowable deduction of £120. (The net cost to Steve)

(d) (a) The employer pays a percentage of her salary into the scheme, but Genna does not

5 Preparing income tax computations

5.1

	£
Pension Income	27,000
Gross dividends	1,350
	28,350
Personal allowance	10,235
Taxable income	18,115
Tax: general income	
16,765 x 20%	3,353
dividends	
1,350 x 10%	135
Tax liability	3,488

Personal allowance working:

Total Income	£28,350
Less grossed-up gift aid payments (£400 x 100/80)	£ 500
Income for comparison with limit	£27,850

His age-related allowance would be calculated as follows:

Age-related allowance – born before 6/4/1938	£10,660
Less restriction 50% x (£27,850 – £27,000)	£425
Allowance	£10,235

5.2

		True	False
(a)	Payments on account relating to a tax year are paid on 31 January in the tax year, and on 31 July following the tax year	✔	
(b)	The final payment of income tax relating to a tax year is paid on 31 October following the end of the tax year		✔
(c)	If a taxpayer is late paying income tax then he will either be subject to a penalty or interest, but not both		✔
(d)	If a tax return is submitted on 31 March following the end of the tax year, the taxpayer would be subject to a penalty of £150		✔
(e)	If a tax return is submitted on 31 May (approximately 14 months after the end of the tax year), the taxpayer would be subject to a penalty of £100 plus a daily penalty	✔	
(f)	Late payment of a final balancing payment of income tax by more than 30 days will be subject to a penalty of 5% of the tax due	✔	

5.3

		True	False
(a)	Charlie did nothing wrong as the tax on dividends has already been deducted		✔
(b)	Charlie did nothing wrong as dividends are exempt from income tax		✔
(c)	Charlie will be subject to a penalty of between 30% and 100% of the dividend income that he has not declared		✔
(d)	Charlie will be subject to a penalty of between 30% and 100% of the extra income tax that is due on the dividends	✔	
(e)	Charlie cannot be charged a penalty if it is his first offence		✔

5.4

Workings	
	£
Salary	45,000
Car benefit £22,000 x (12% + 12% + 3%)	5,940
Fuel Benefit £21,700 x 27%	5,859
Sub total	56,799
Personal allowance	10,000
Taxable income	46,799
Tax at 20%: Band £31,865 + (1,600 x 100/80) = 33,865 x 20%	6,773
Tax at 40%: (£46,799 − £33,865) x 40%	5,174
Total tax liability	11,946

5.5

HM Revenue & Customs

Employment
Tax year 6 April 2013 to 5 April 2014

Your name

Mike

Your Unique Taxpayer Reference (UTR)

Complete an *Employment* page for each employment or directorship

1 Pay from this employment – the total from your
P45 or P60 - *before tax was taken off*

£ 4 5 0 0 0 · 0 0

2 UK tax taken off pay in box 1

£ · 0 0

3 Tips and other payments not on your P60
- *read the Employment notes*

£ · 0 0

4 PAYE tax reference of your employer (on your P45/P60)

/

5 Your employer's name

6 If you were a company director, put 'X' in the box

7 And, if the company was a close company, put 'X'
in the box

8 If you are a part-time teacher in England or Wales and
are on the Repayment of Teachers' Loans Scheme for
this employment, put 'X' in the box

Benefits from your employment - use your form P11D (or equivalent information)

9 Company cars and vans
- *the total 'cash equivalent' amount*

£ 2 8 8 0 · 0 0

10 Fuel for company cars and vans
- *the total 'cash equivalent' amount*

£ 3 9 0 6 · 0 0

11 Private medical and dental insurance
- *the total 'cash equivalent' amount*

£ · 0 0

12 Vouchers, credit cards and excess mileage allowance

£ · 0 0

13 Goods and other assets provided by your employer
- *the total value or amount*

£ · 0 0

14 Accommodation provided by your employer
- *the total value or amount*

£ · 0 0

15 Other benefits (including interest-free and low
interest loans) - *the total 'cash equivalent' amount*

£ 1 9 5 · 0 0

16 Expenses payments received and balancing charges

£ · 0 0

Employment expenses

17 Business travel and subsistence expenses

£ · 0 0

18 Fixed deductions for expenses

£ · 0 0

19 Professional fees and subscriptions

£ 2 0 0 · 0 0

20 Other expenses and capital allowances

£ · 0 0

ⓘ Share schemes, employment lump sums, compensation, deductions and Seafarers' Earnings Deduction are on the
Additional information pages enclosed in the tax return pack.

5.6

	£
Employment Income	91,500
Gross dividends	17,500
	109,000
Personal allowance	6,250
Taxable income	102,750
General income:	
(31,865 + 1,500) x 20%	6,673
(85,250* – 33,365) x 40%	20,754
Dividend income	
17,500 x 32.5%	5,687
Tax liability	33,114

Workings:

Adjusted net income: £91,500 + £17,500 – £1,500 = £107,500

Personal alllowance: £10,000 – 50% x (£107,500 – £100,000) = £6,250

* General income: £91,500 – £6,250 = £85,250

6   Capital gains tax – the main principles

6.1

		Actual Proceeds Used	Deemed proceeds used	No gain or loss basis
(a)	Father gives an asset to his son		✔	
(b)	Wife sells an asset to her husband			✔
(c)	Simon gives an asset to his friend		✔	
(d)	Margaret sells an asset to her cousin for £15,000 when the market value is £40,000	✔		
(e)	Brian gives an asset to his civil partner, Dave			✔

6.2   £4,190

True: legal fees are an allowable deduction where they relate to the purchase or sale of an asset.

6.3

		True	False
(a)	The annual exemption is applied after capital losses are deducted.	✔	
(b)	Capital losses from the same year cannot safeguard the annual exemption.	✔	
(c)	Capital gains are taxed at 28% for higher rate tax payers.	✔	
(d)	Capital losses can be set against gains of the previous tax year.		✔
(e)	Capital losses brought forward can safeguard the annual exemption when offset against current year gains.	✔	

6.4   **(a)**   The gain on the asset is **£12,500**

(b)   The amount of loss that will be relieved is **£1,500**

(c)   The capital gains tax payable is **£0**

(d)   The loss to be carried forward to the next tax year is **£2,500**

6.5

Asset	Exempt	Chargeable
Antique furniture valued at £30,000		✔
Principal private residence	✔	
Clock	✔	
Shares		✔
Holiday home		✔
Government securities	✔	
Vintage car	✔	
Land		✔

7 Capital gains tax – some special rules

7.1 **(a)**

Occupation / Deemed Occupation	Non-occupation
1/1/2000 - 31/12/2002 (36 months)	
1/1/2003 - 31/12/2003 (12 months)	
1/1/2004 - 30/6/2005 (18 months)	
1/7/2005 - 31/12/2011 (78 months)	1/1/2012 - 30/6/2013 (18 months)
1/7/2013 - 1/1/2015 (18 months)	

(b) Chargeable gain is £8,000 ((£205,000 – £125,000) x 18/180)

7.2

Asset	Sale proceeds	Cost	Statement
1	£4,000	£7,000	Sale proceeds to be £6,000
2	£14,000	£8,000	Calculate gain as normal
3	£8,000	£3,000	Chattel marginal relief applies
4	£3,000	£5,000	Exempt asset
5	£15,000	£21,000	Calculate loss as normal

7.3

	Number of shares	£
October 2000	20,000	100,000
Bonus	800	0
Sub total	20,800	100,000
Disposal	8,000	38,462
Pool balance	12,800	61,538
Proceeds		72,000
Cost		38,462
Gain		33,538

7.4

HM Revenue & Customs

Capital gains summary
Tax year 6 April 2013 to 5 April 2014

1 Your name	2 Your Unique Taxpayer Reference (UTR)
B O B	

Summary of your enclosed computations

Please read the *Capital gains summary notes* before filling in this section. **You must enclose your computations, including details of each gain or loss, as well as filling in the boxes.**

ℹ To get notes and helpsheets that will help you fill in this form, go to hmrc.gov.uk/selfassessmentforms

3 Total gains *(Boxes 21 + 27 + 33 + 34)*
£ 104000 · 0 0

4 Gains qualifying for Entrepreneurs' Relief (but excluding gains deferred from before 23 June 2010) – *read the notes*
£ · 0 0

5 Gains invested under Seed Enterprise Investment Scheme and qualifying for exemption – *read the notes*
£ · 0 0

6 Total losses of the year – *enter '0' if there are none*
£ 15000 · 0 0

7 Losses brought forward and used in the year
£ · 0 0

8 Adjustment to Capital Gains Tax – *read the notes*
£ ▬ · 0 0

9 Additional liability for non-resident or dual resident trusts
£ · 0 0

10 Losses available to be carried forward to later years
£ · 0 0

11 Losses used against an earlier year's gain (special circumstances apply – *read the notes*)
£ · 0 0

12 Losses used against income – amount claimed against 2013-14 income – *read the notes*
£ · 0 0

13 Amount in box 12 relating to shares to which Enterprise Investment Scheme/Seed Enterprise Investment Scheme relief is attributable
£ · 0 0

14 Losses used against income – amount claimed against 2012-13 income – *read the notes*
£ · 0 0

15 Amount in box 14 relating to shares to which Enterprise Investment Scheme/Seed Enterprise Investment Scheme relief is attributable
£ · 0 0

16 Income losses of 2013-14 set against gains
£ · 0 0

17 Deferred gains from before 23 June 2010 qualifying for Entrepreneurs' Relief
£ · 0 0

Listed shares and securities

18 Number of disposals - *read the notes*

`2`

19 Disposal proceeds

£ `3 8 0 0 0 · 0 0`

20 Allowable costs (including purchase price)

£ `4 5 0 0 0 · 0 0`

21 Gains in the year, before losses

£ `8 0 0 0 · 0 0`

22 If you are making any claim or election, put 'X' in the box

23 If your computations include any estimates or valuations, put 'X' in the box

Unlisted shares and securities

24 Number of disposals - *read the notes*

`1`

25 Disposal proceeds

£ `4 8 0 0 0 · 0 0`

26 Allowable costs (including purchase price)

£ `3 2 0 0 0 · 0 0`

27 Gains in the year, before losses

£ `1 6 0 0 0 · 0 0`

28 If you are making any claim or election, put 'X' in the box

29 If your computations include any estimates or valuations, put 'X' in the box

Property and other assets and gains

30 Number of disposals

`1`

31 Disposal proceeds

£ `2 3 0 0 0 0 · 0 0`

32 Allowable costs (including purchase price)

£ `1 5 0 0 0 0 · 0 0`

33 Gains in the year, before losses

£ `8 0 0 0 0 · 0 0`

34 Attributed gains where personal losses cannot be set off

£ `· 0 0`

35 If you are making any claim or election, put 'X' in the box

36 If your computations include any estimates or valuations, put 'X' in the box

---

7.5 **(a)** The gain on the painting is **£9,100**

(b) The gain on the land is **£5,200**

(c) The result of the sale of the holiday cottage is a **loss** of **£3,000**

(d) The capital gains tax payable is **£84**

Practice
assessment 1

Task 1 (a)

What scale charge precentage would be applied for petrol cars with the following CO_2 emissions?

    (1)   99 g/km

    (2)   140 g/km

    (3)   171 g/km

    (4)   241 g/km

(b)

Steve was provided with a second hand company car on 6 November 2014. It cost the company £9,000, but the list price of this car when bought new was £16,000. The car has a CO_2 emission of 151g/km, and has a diesel engine. The company pays for all running costs, except private fuel.

    (1)   The cost of the car used in the benefit in kind computation is

    £ _____

    (2)   The percentage used in the benefit in kind computation is

    _____ %

    (3)   The assessable benefit for Steve relating to the car for 2014/15 is

    £ _____

Task 2(a)

(1)   When accommodation is purchased by an employer, what is the value of the property above which an additional benefit is applied?

✔

(a) £50,000	
(b) £75,000	
(c) £100,000	
(d) £125,000	
(e) £150,000	

(2)   Would the following situations be treated as being job-related where no accommodation benefit arises?

✔

	Yes	No
(a) House provided for a finance director		
(b) House provided by employer for librarian working for local authority		
(c) Flat in nursing home provided for an on-site nursing manager		

(3)   Sian was provided with accommodation in the form of a flat that the employer purchased for £125,000. It is not job related. The flat has an annual value £6,300. The employer also bought furniture for the flat, costing £2,000. Assume that the HMRC official interest rate is 3.25%. Her taxable benefit is:

✔

(a) £6,300	
(b) £8,300	
(c) £8,325	
(d) £10,762	
(e) £12,362	

continued

Task 2(b)

Using the following table, analyse the benefits into those that are exempt from tax, and those that are taxable.

Description	Exempt	Taxable
Interest-free loans not exceeding £10,000		
Cash payment to employee to help with childcare costs		
Employer contributions to company pension scheme		
Free meals in a staff restaurant only available to senior managers		
Performance related bonus payment		
Provision of one mobile telephone and its running costs		
Holiday pay		
Use of a bicycle and helmet to commute to work		
Childcare vouchers up to £55 per week for basic rate taxpayers		

Task 3(a)

Charlie has two properties in addition to his home, details of which are as follows:

Two bedroom house:

(1)   This unfurnished house is rented out for £850 per month. The property was occupied this tax year until 31 January when the tenants moved out, with the rent paid up to date. The property was let again from 1 March at a rent of £900 per month.

(2)   Charlie paid £1510 for redecoration and repainting in February. He also spent £1,200 adding a porch to the house.

(3)   The only other expense paid by Charlie on the house was 12% management charge to the agent on rent received.

One bedroom flat:

(1)   This furnished flat is rented out for £490 per month. The property was rented all tax year.

(2)   Charlie paid council tax and water rates on the flat, totalling £1,160 for the period that the flat was occupied. He also paid buildings and contents insurance of £370 for the year.

Calculate the profit or loss made on each property, using the following table.

	Two bedroom house £	One bedroom flat £
Income		
Expenses:		

(b)

Mike rents a furnished room in his own house to a lodger for £260 per week, including breakfast and an evening meal. Heating the room costs Mike £170 for the year, and food for the lodger's meals costs £28 per week.

(1) Calculate the assessable amount for the tax year, based on

    (a) claiming rent a room relief, and

    (b) preparing a normal rental income computation

using the following table.

	Claiming rent a room relief £	**Normal rental income computation** £
Income	13,520	13,520
Allowable deductions:		

(2) Complete the following sentence:

To pay the minimum income tax, Mike should **claim / not claim** rent a room relief.

Task 4(a)

Kerry has received the amounts shown on the following table from various investments. Complete the table to show the assessable amounts and the amounts of tax that are treated as having been paid.

Investment	Amount Received £	Assessable Amount £	Tax treated as paid £
Building Society Account	1,500		
Dividends from UK Cos.	4,950		
Stocks & Shares NISA	190		
Local authority loan interest	1,600		
Totals	8,240		

(b)

Complete the following table to show the maximum investment in a cash NISA that an individual can make from July 2014 assuming no investment in a stocks and shares NISA.

Cash NISA limit	

Task 5

Kate provides you with the following information that relates to her income for the tax year 2014/15.

- Annual salary was £109,600 from 1 January 2014. She received a pay rise of 2% from 1 January 2015.

- She received an interest free loan from her employer. The assessable benefit in kind has been calculated at £1,160.

- She received an allowance of £5,000 from her employer to entertain clients during the tax year, but she actually spent £7,500 entertaining clients.

- She paid £8,000 into a personal pension scheme. Her employer did not make any contributions.

- She received £1,600 bank interest during the tax year.

- She received dividends totalling £3,150 during the tax year.

Complete the following table to calculate the total taxable income for Kate. Do not use brackets or minus signs.

	£
Salary	
Benefit in kind loan	
Entertaining clients	
Personal pension	
Bank interest	
Dividend income	
Personal allowance	
Taxable income	

Task 6(a)

James, who is 80 years old, had pension income of £102,000 and received bank interest of £600 (net).

He paid £800 (net) to charities under the gift aid scheme.

Calculate his total income tax liability (ie before deduction of tax paid) for the tax year, using the table given below.

	£
Pension Income	
Bank Interest	
Personal Allowance	
Taxable Income	
Tax:	

continued

(b)

The company that you work for is changing from paying mileage allowances for staff using their own cars to providing pool cars for business travel.

Until now the company has paid 50p per mile for all business journeys in employees' own cars. Under the new system, pool cars will be available at the workplace for employees to use for business journeys only. Staff will need to fill up the car that they are using with petrol when necessary, and submit a claim for reimbursement from the company. All staff have already been told about the new system, but are not aware of any tax implications.

Required:

Write an email to all staff to compare the tax implications of the new scheme for staff with the previous scheme.

email
from:
to:
subject:
date:

Task 7

It is January 2015. John is a new client and a higher rate taxpayer. He has just told you that he did not include on the relevant tax return £5,000 income that he received in 2012/13. He doesn't know whether it is too late to notify HMRC about the omission, and what the consequences of telling HMRC or keeping quiet could be.

Explain the relevant deadlines and the main implications of either notifying HMRC now or of failing to notify HMRC.

Task 8

Simon rents out one furnished property. He claims wear and tear allowance. The following is a statement compiled from his accounting records relating to the tax year.

	£	£
Rental Income Receivable		10,000
less expenditure:		
Council Tax	720	
Water Rates	260	
Insurance	280	
Cost of replacement carpets	2,100	
Depreciation of Furniture	900	
Managing Agent's Charges	800	
	5,060	
Profit		4,940

Required:

(a) Calculate the assessable property income for Simon, using the following table.

	£	£
Income		
Expenditure:		
Assessable Income		

(b) Complete page UKP2 of the UK Property supplementary pages, (the 2013/14 version is reproduced on the opposite page) for Simon.

Property income

Do not include furnished holiday lettings, Real Estate Investment Trust or Property Authorised Investment Funds dividends/distributions here.

20 Total rents and other income from property

£ ⬚⬚⬚⬚⬚⬚⬚⬚⬚ . 0 0

21 Tax taken off any income in box 20 – *read the notes*

£ ⬚⬚⬚⬚⬚⬚⬚⬚⬚ . 0 0

22 Premiums for the grant of a lease – from box E on the Working Sheet – *read the notes*

£ ⬚⬚⬚⬚⬚⬚⬚⬚⬚ . 0 0

23 Reverse premiums and inducements

£ ⬚⬚⬚⬚⬚⬚⬚⬚⬚ . 0 0

Property expenses

24 Rent, rates, insurance, ground rents etc.

£ ⬚⬚⬚⬚⬚⬚⬚⬚⬚ . 0 0

25 Property repairs and maintenance

£ ⬚⬚⬚⬚⬚⬚⬚⬚⬚ . 0 0

26 Loan interest and other financial costs

£ ⬚⬚⬚⬚⬚⬚⬚⬚⬚ . 0 0

27 Legal, management and other professional fees

£ ⬚⬚⬚⬚⬚⬚⬚⬚⬚ . 0 0

28 Costs of services provided, including wages

£ ⬚⬚⬚⬚⬚⬚⬚⬚⬚ . 0 0

29 Other allowable property expenses

£ ⬚⬚⬚⬚⬚⬚⬚⬚⬚ . 0 0

Calculating your taxable profit or loss

30 Private use adjustment – *read the notes*

£ ⬚⬚⬚⬚⬚⬚⬚⬚⬚ . 0 0

31 Balancing charges – *read the notes*

£ ⬚⬚⬚⬚⬚⬚⬚⬚⬚ . 0 0

32 Annual Investment Allowance

£ ⬚⬚⬚⬚⬚⬚⬚⬚⬚ . 0 0

33 Business Premises Renovation Allowance (Assisted Areas only) – *read the notes*

£ ⬚⬚⬚⬚⬚⬚⬚⬚⬚ . 0 0

34 All other capital allowances

£ ⬚⬚⬚⬚⬚⬚⬚⬚⬚ . 0 0

35 Landlord's Energy Saving Allowance

£ ⬚⬚⬚⬚⬚⬚⬚⬚⬚ . 0 0

36 10% wear and tear allowance – *for furnished residential accommodation only*

£ ⬚⬚⬚⬚⬚⬚⬚⬚⬚ . 0 0

37 Rent a Room exempt amount

£ ⬚⬚⬚⬚⬚ . 0 0

38 Adjusted profit for the year – from box O on the Working Sheet – *read the notes*

£ ⬚⬚⬚⬚⬚⬚⬚⬚⬚ . 0 0

39 Loss brought forward used against this year's profits

£ ⬚⬚⬚⬚⬚⬚⬚⬚⬚ . 0 0

40 Taxable profit for the year (box 38 minus box 39)

£ ⬚⬚⬚⬚⬚⬚⬚⬚⬚ . 0 0

41 Adjusted loss for the year – from box O on the Working Sheet – *read the notes*

£ ⬚⬚⬚⬚⬚⬚⬚⬚⬚ . 0 0

42 Loss set off against 2013-14 total income – *this will be unusual – read the notes*

£ ⬚⬚⬚⬚⬚⬚⬚⬚⬚ . 0 0

43 Loss to carry forward to following year, including unused losses brought forward

£ ⬚⬚⬚⬚⬚⬚⬚⬚⬚ . 0 0

Task 9(a)

For each statement, tick the appropriate box.

✔

	Actual Proceeds Used	Deemed proceeds used	No gain or loss basis
(1) Dave gives an asset to his father			
(2) Peter sells an asset to his friend			
(3) Simon gives an asset to his friend			

(b)

John has a capital loss brought forward of £2,500. He has taxable income for the year of £25,000.

He sold an asset during the tax year for £21,000. He had been left the asset when his grandfather died. His grandfather had paid £6,000 for the asset, and it was valued at £9,500 at the time of death.

Complete the following sentences:

(1) The gain on the asset is £

(2) The amount of loss that will be relieved is £

(3) The capital gains tax payable is £

(4) The loss to be carried forward to the next tax year is £

(c)

Complete the following table to show which assets are exempt from capital gains tax and which are chargeable.

✔

Asset	Exempt	Chargeable
Land		
Principal private residence		
Antique painting valued at £20,000		
Unquoted shares		
Caravan		
Government securities		
Classic car		
Horse		

Task 10

Pam bought 25,000 shares in Lester Ltd for £5 per share in October 2000. In April 2005 she took up a rights issue of 3 for 5 at £4 per share. In January 2015, Pam sold 10,000 shares for £8 per share.

Clearly showing the balance of shares, and their value, to carry forward calculate the gain made on these shares. All workings must be shown in your calculations.

Task 11(a)

Roger bought a house on 1 January 1999. He lived in the house until 31 December 2002 when he moved to Aberdeen to take up a job, where he stayed until 30 June 2006, while renting out his own house. He then moved back into his own house from 1 July 2006 until 31 December 2010, when he moved to a new home and put the house on the market. The house was eventually sold on 1 March 2015.

Which periods are treated as occupied and which are not?

Occupation / Deemed Occupation	Non-occupation

(b)

State which of the following statements are true and which are false: ✔

		True	False
(1)	The annual exemption is applied before current year capital losses are deducted, but after brought forward capital losses		
(2)	Capital losses brought forward cannot safeguard the annual exemption		
(3)	Capital gains are taxed at 18% for all taxpayers		
(4)	Capital losses can be set against income of the previous tax year		

Practice assessment 2

Task 1

Miranda had the use of two company cars during 2014/15. The company paid for all the running costs of the cars, including all fuel.

Details of the cars are as follows:

Car	Period of use	List price £	Cost £	CO₂ emission	Type of engine
Ford	5 months of the tax year	28,500	27,600	139 g/km	Petrol
Kia	7 months of the tax year	26,600	26,600	124 g/km	Diesel

Complete the following table to show Miranda's taxable benefit in kind for the cars for 2014/15. Show amounts in whole pounds.

Car		%	£
Ford	Scale charge percentage		
	Taxable benefit on provision of the car		
	Taxable benefit on provision of fuel		
Kia	Scale charge percentage		
	Taxable benefit on provision of the car		
	Taxable benefit on provision of fuel		
Total taxable benefit			

Task 2(a)

Indicate whether each of the following will or will not result in an assessable benefit in kind for the employee by ticking the appropriate box.

The following are provided by the employer to the employee	Assessable benefit in kind	Not assessable benefit in kind
Use of a bicycle and helmet to commute to work		
Subscription to gym that is also used by non-employees		
Allowance of £5 per night for incidental costs while staying away from home on business		
Relocation costs of £5,000 when required to move house by the employer		

(b)

Robert was provided with the following by his employer during the tax year:

- A new computer games console to use at home for the whole tax year. This cost the employer £350, and remains the employer's property. By the end of the tax year the console was valued at £100.

- An interest free loan of £14,000 at the start of the tax year. Robert repaid £6,000 on 6th January 2015, but made no other repayments.

- Mileage allowance of 60p per mile for business journeys using Robert's own car. Robert claimed for trips totalling 13,000 miles.

Complete the following table to show the total assessable benefits (if any).

	Assessable amount £
Use of computer games console	
Interest free loan	
Mileage allowance	

Task 3(a)

Julian has a furnished house that he lets for £550 per calendar month. His expenditure regarding the house was as follows:

Resurfacing garden path	£200
Building and contents insurance:	
Year to 31 December 2014	£336
Year to 31 December 2015	£360
Insurance against irrecoverable rent	
Year to 31 March 2015	£120
Agent's management charge	£792
Repairing central heating	£250

Complete the following table to show the assessable profit on the property.

	£
Income	
Expenditure:	
Resurfacing path	
Building and contents insurance	
Irrecoverable rent insurance	
Agent's management charges	
Repairs to central heating	
Wear and tear	
PROFIT	

(b)

Megan has income from both furnished holiday lettings and from normal rental income. The following were her profits and losses for each type of income for the last few years.

Details	Profit £	Loss £
2012/13 Holiday lettings		2,800
2012/13 Other property income	7,900	
2013/14 Holiday lettings	3,000	
2013/14 Other property income		4,300
2014/15 Holiday lettings	6,750	
2014/15 Other property income	10,500	

Complete the following table to show the loss relieved and the total assessable property income for each tax year. Do not use brackets or minus signs.

	2012/13 £	2013/14 £	2014/15 £
Loss relieved			
Total assessable property income			

Task 4

Brian, who is 47 years old, receives interest from a NISA, interest from a bank account and dividends from shares. His other income (before deducting personal allowance) was £35,000.

Calculate the assessable amount, the tax deducted at source and any additional tax payable for each type of income shown in the table below. Show answers in pounds and pence.

Income	Amount received £	Assessable amount £	Tax deducted at source £	Additional tax payable £
Interest from NISA	1,400			
Interest from Bank	5,500			
Dividends	1,800			

Task 5

Karen provides you with the following information that relates to her income for the tax year 2014/15.

- Annual salary is £94,500. She received a bonus of £4,000 in August 2014.
- She lives in a flat owned by her employer. The assessable benefit in kind has been calculated at £6,455.
- She paid £1,900 entertaining clients during the tax year and this was reimbursed by her employer.
- She paid 5% of her basic salary into a company pension scheme, and her employer contributed 9% of her basic salary into the same scheme.
- She contributed £1,600 (net) to charities under the gift aid scheme.
- She received dividends totalling £3,150 during the tax year.

Complete the following table to calculate the total taxable income for Karen. Do not use brackets or minus signs.

	£
Basic salary	
Bonus	
Benefit in kind accommodation	
Benefit in kind entertaining	
Employer's pension contribution	
Employee's pension contribution	
Gift aid payment	
Dividend income	
Personal allowance	
Taxable income	

Task 6

Robin had the following income for the tax year:

Employment income	£32,000
Property income	£10,100
Interest received from Building Society	£3,300
Dividends received	£3,690

(a)

Calculate Robin's income tax liability for the tax year, using the following table for your workings and answer.

(b)

Robin intends to start paying £100 per month from his bank account to a charity. The charity has asked whether he would like to make the payment under the gift aid scheme. Robin does not understand the implications of doing this.

Explain to Robin the implications for him and the charity of making the payments under the gift aid scheme.

Task 7

A new client is concerned that he has made a late self assessment payment to HMRC.

The amount due on 31 January 2015 was made up of:

Balancing payment for 2013/14	£5,100
Payment on account for 2014/15	£9,300
Total	£14,400

This amount was paid in full on 31 May 2015.

Explain how any interest and / or penalties will be calculated on the above late payment.

Task 8

Vikram has provided the following information regarding his employment in the tax year:

Gross pay   £28,350

Assessable amounts for benefits in kind:
Company car   £4,650
Fuel for company car   £6,900
Interest free loan   £350

Vikram paid £780 for hotel costs while on business and this was reimbursed by his employer. The employer does not hold an HMRC dispensation.

Vikram also paid £200 for a professional subscription, but this was not reimbursed by his employer.

Complete, as far as possible, the extract from page E1 of the tax return shown on the next page for Vikram.

 **HM Revenue & Customs**

Employment
Tax year 6 April 2013 to 5 April 2014

Your name

Your Unique Taxpayer Reference (UTR)

Complete an *Employment* page for each employment or directorship

1 Pay from this employment – the total from your P45 or P60 – *before tax was taken off*

£ · 0 0

2 UK tax taken off pay in box 1

£ · 0 0

3 Tips and other payments not on your P60
– *read the Employment notes*

£ · 0 0

4 PAYE tax reference of your employer (on your P45/P60)

/

5 Your employer's name

6 If you were a company director, put 'X' in the box

7 And, if the company was a close company, put 'X' in the box

8 If you are a part-time teacher in England or Wales and are on the Repayment of Teachers' Loans Scheme for this employment, put 'X' in the box

Benefits from your employment – use your form P11D (or equivalent information)

9 Company cars and vans
– *the total 'cash equivalent' amount*

£ · 0 0

10 Fuel for company cars and vans
– *the total 'cash equivalent' amount*

£ · 0 0

11 Private medical and dental insurance
– *the total 'cash equivalent' amount*

£ · 0 0

12 Vouchers, credit cards and excess mileage allowance

£ · 0 0

13 Goods and other assets provided by your employer
– *the total value or amount*

£ · 0 0

14 Accommodation provided by your employer
– *the total value or amount*

£ · 0 0

15 Other benefits (including interest-free and low interest loans) – *the total 'cash equivalent' amount*

£ · 0 0

16 Expenses payments received and balancing charges

£ · 0 0

Employment expenses

17 Business travel and subsistence expenses

£ · 0 0

18 Fixed deductions for expenses

£ · 0 0

19 Professional fees and subscriptions

£ · 0 0

20 Other expenses and capital allowances

£ · 0 0

ⓘ **Share schemes, employment lump sums, compensation, deductions and Seafarers' Earnings Deduction** are on the *Additional information* pages enclosed in the tax return pack.

SA102 2014   Page E 1   HMRC 12/13

Task 9(a)

Indicate whether each of the following statements is true or false.

✔

	True	False
A chattel bought and sold for less than £6,000 is exempt from capital gains tax		
Transfers between spouses are carried out on a 'no gain, no loss' basis		
Capital gains tax will be incurred on the increase in value of investments between the date of purchase and the date of the owners' death		
Mechanical chattels (for example clocks) owned for personal use are exempt from capital gains tax		

(b)

Josie bought a painting for £14,000 and spent £3,000 having it restored and £800 insuring it. She sold it for £16,000.

Select the capital gain or loss on disposal from the following:

✔

Zero (exempt asset)	
Gain of £2,000	
Loss of £1,000	
Loss of £1,800	

(c)

Jack's grandfather, John, bought an asset for £6,600. Some years later John died and left the asset to Jack in his will. The asset was valued at £9,400 at that time.

Recently, Jack sold the asset to his sister, Jill for £6,000 when it was valued at £11,000.

Complete the following table to calculate the gain or loss when Jack sold the asset to Jill. Use a minus sign to denote a loss.

	£
Proceeds or deemed proceeds	
Cost or deemed cost	
Gain or loss	

Task 10

Ken bought 800 shares in Kandle Ltd for £3,000 in April 2003. In May 2009 he bought a further 1,200 shares for £3.90 each. In December 2010 a rights issue of 1 for 5 at £2.00 per share was offered, and Ken took up the offer.

Ken sold 500 shares on 11 November 2014 for a total of £3,000. On 23 December 2014 he purchased a further 100 shares for £6.30 each.

Clearly showing the balance of shares and their value to carry forward, calculate the gain made on the sale of shares that occurred in 2014/15.

Task 11(a)

Richard bought a house on 1 January 2004 for £125,000 to use as a holiday home. He sold the house on 30 June 2014 for £198,000.

During the period of ownership the following occurred:

Period	
1/1/2004 - 31/3/2008	Used as a holiday home
1/4/2008 - 31/12/2008	Left empty as Richard worked abroad
1/1/2009 - 31/12/2011	Richard lived in the house as his main residence
1/1/2012 - 30/6/2014	Richard moved to a new house

Complete the following table:

Total period of ownership in months	
Period of actual occupation in months	
Period of deemed occupation in months	
Chargeable gain on the sale of the house	£

(b)

Complete the table below to indicate the relief of capital losses in 2014/15 for the following taxpayers.

	Capital Loss 2013/14 £	Capital Loss 2014/15 £	Capital Gain 2014/15 £	Amount of Loss to be relieved 2014/15 £	Amount of Loss carried forward £
Brian	6,900	4,500	15,000		
Colin	0	6,900	15,000		
Denise	6,900	0	15,000		

Practice assessment 3

Task 1

Dirk is a senior manager in the defence industry. During the tax year he was provided with the following company cars:

From the start of the tax year until 30 June he was provided with a Jaguar. It was purchased for £41,000 second hand, and had a list price of £52,000. Its emissions were 152 g/km and it was powered by a petrol engine.

Following a promotion for Dirk, the Jaguar was replaced with a new diesel powered Range Rover on 1 July. This car had a list price of £72,000. The company believed that Dirk's new role placed him at increased risk of a terrorism attack, and paid £25,000 for the Range Rover to be equipped with bullet resistant glass and strengthened bodywork. The emissions of the car were 230 g/km. On 1 December the car was fitted with passengers' televisions so that Dirk's family could be entertained on long trips. This cost the company £1,200.

Complete the following table to show the 2014/15 benefit in kind arising from the use of these cars. Ignore any benefit arising from private fuel.

Car	Percentage applicable based on CO$_2$ emissions %	Cost of car used in benefit calculation £	Benefit in kind £
Jaguar			
Range Rover			
Total			

Task 2(a)

Place a tick in the appropriate column of the table below to show whether each of the items listed would or would not result in an assessable benefit in kind for an employee.

✔

The following are provided by the employer to the employee	Benefit in kind	No benefit in kind
Use of a company credit card to pay for the entertainment of customers (with approval of the employer)		
Mileage payment for use of employee's own motorcycle for business purposes at a rate of 24p per mile		
Petrol for travel from home to work in a company car		
Training costs including course and examination fees for accountancy trainee undertaking AAT course		

(b)

Calculate the assessable benefit in kind (in whole pounds) for each of the following:

	Benefit £
On 6 April an employee was provided with an interest free loan of £15,000. During the tax year he made three repayments, each of £2,000. The remainder of the loan was still outstanding at the end of the tax year.	
On 6 April an employee was allowed the use of a home cinema system that had previously been used by the company. The home cinema had originally cost the company £1,500, but its market value on 6 April was £1,000.	

continued

Task 2(c)

Using the following table, analyse the benefits into those that are exempt from tax, and those that are taxable.

Description	Exempt	Taxable
Provision of a chauffeur for business and private journeys		
Long service award in cash for employee with 10 year's service		
Counselling services		
Free meals in a staff restaurant available to all staff		
Provision of free UK health insurance		

(d)

Tick the appropriate box to show whether each of the following situations would increase or reduce an employee's tax liability under the approved mileage allowance payments scheme.

Business mileage and rate paid	Increase tax liability	Reduce tax liability
5,000 miles at 50p per mile		
15,000 miles at 45p per mile		
15,000 miles at 38p per mile		
20,000 miles at 25p per mile		

Task 3(a)

Analyse the following expenses into whether they are an allowable deduction in calculating UK property income or not by ticking the appropriate column.

✔

	Allowable deduction	Not an allowable deduction
Depreciation of property		
Monthly repayment of mortgage capital		
Advertising for tenants		
Repainting windows		
Insurance against irrecoverable rent		
Installing central heating		
Capital allowances related to holiday lettings		

(b)

Indicate with a tick whether each of the following statements related to property income is true or false.

✔

	True	False
If a taxpayer is claiming rent a room relief he cannot claim any other deductions from the rental income		
The time limit to claim rent a room relief is one year after the due date for the online tax return		

(c)

Jessica has a furnished cottage that she rents out to holiday makers. During the tax year it was available for letting from 1 May until 31 October. It was unoccupied for two weeks during this period.

Does this qualify as a furnished holiday letting? Tick one statement.

✔

Statement	
Yes, this qualifies	
No, this doesn't qualify only because it was not actually let for long enough	
No, this doesn't qualify only because it wasn't available for letting for long enough	
No, this doesn't qualify because it was neither available nor actually let for long enough	

Task 4(a)

Kerry has received the amounts shown on the following table from various investments. Complete the table to show the assessable amounts and the amounts of tax that are treated as having been paid.

Investment	Amount Received £	Assessable Amount £	Tax treated as paid £
Bank deposit account	1,600		
Cash NISA	270		
Government stocks (gilts)	1,200		
Totals	3,070		

(b)

Jo is a taxpayer whose amount of general income means that she pays tax at the additional rate. She received £3,600 in UK dividends.

Complete the following table in respect of the dividend income:

	Assessable amount £	Total tax liability £
Dividends received of £3,600		

Task 5

Ken provides you with the following information that relates to his income for the tax year 2014/15.

- Ken was born in August 1945.
- Annual total pension was £19,650.
- He received interest from a NISA of £780.
- He paid £1,360 to charities under the gift aid scheme during the tax year.
- He received £3,200 bank interest during the tax year.
- He received dividends totalling £4,950 during the tax year.

Complete the following table to calculate the total taxable income for Ken. Do not use brackets or minus signs.

	£
Pension	
NISA interest	
Bank interest	
Dividend income	
Gift aid payments	
Total income	
Personal allowance	
Taxable income	

Task 6(a)

During the tax year, Jennifer had employment income of £127,500 and received dividends of £900 (net).

She paid £16,000 (net) into a personal pension scheme.

Calculate her total income tax liability (i.e. before deduction of tax paid), using the blank table given below.

(b)

The company that you work for has recently arranged for payroll giving to be available for all staff so that they can donate to charities.

Write an email to all staff that explains how payroll giving works and compares it with the gift aid scheme.

| **email** |
| from: |
| to: |
| subject: |
| date: |

Task 7

It is September 2015.

A new client has approached you for information about his future tax payments, and is worried about what will happen if he cannot afford to pay these amounts.

The client has provided you with the following information about the self assessment payments that he has already made:

Paid 31 January 2015:

2013/14 Balancing payment £13,250 + First payment on account for 2014/15 £11,625

= Total £24,875.

Paid 31 July 2015:

Second payment on account for 2014/15 £11,625

You have completed the draft tax computations for him for 2014/15 and calculate that the total income tax payable for the tax year will be £26,800. In addition there will be capital gains tax for 2014/15 of £10,250.

Explain the amounts that will be payable on 31 January 2016 and 31 July 2016 and how they are calculated. Also explain briefly the implications of not making these payments when due.

Explanation of amounts payable

Implications of not making payments when due

Task 8

Jack Price is employed by PPP Limited. His P60 for the tax year showed pay of £44,600 and tax deducted of £9,100.

He was provided with a company car with an assessable benefit amount of £3,000 and fuel for private motoring with an assessable amount of £3,030.

He paid out and reclaimed from his employer business travel expenses of £380 during the tax year. The employer does not hold an HMRC dispensation for such payments.

Complete the relevant sections of the Employment tax return page for Jack. The form is reproduced on the next page.

HM Revenue & Customs

Employment
Tax year 6 April 2013 to 5 April 2014

Your name

Your Unique Taxpayer Reference (UTR)

Complete an *Employment* page for each employment or directorship

1 Pay from this employment – the total from your P45 or P60 - *before tax was taken off*

£ ⬚ . 0 0

2 UK tax taken off pay in box 1

£ ⬚ . 0 0

3 Tips and other payments not on your P60 - *read the Employment notes*

£ ⬚ . 0 0

4 PAYE tax reference of your employer (on your P45/P60)

⬚ / ⬚

5 Your employer's name

6 If you were a company director, put 'X' in the box

7 And, if the company was a close company, put 'X' in the box

8 If you are a part-time teacher in England or Wales and are on the Repayment of Teachers' Loans Scheme for this employment, put 'X' in the box

Benefits from your employment - use your form P11D (or equivalent information)

9 Company cars and vans
- *the total 'cash equivalent' amount*

£ ⬚ . 0 0

10 Fuel for company cars and vans
- *the total 'cash equivalent' amount*

£ ⬚ . 0 0

11 Private medical and dental insurance
- *the total 'cash equivalent' amount*

£ ⬚ . 0 0

12 Vouchers, credit cards and excess mileage allowance

£ ⬚ . 0 0

13 Goods and other assets provided by your employer
- *the total value or amount*

£ ⬚ . 0 0

14 Accommodation provided by your employer
- *the total value or amount*

£ ⬚ . 0 0

15 Other benefits (including interest-free and low interest loans) - *the total 'cash equivalent' amount*

£ ⬚ . 0 0

16 Expenses payments received and balancing charges

£ ⬚ . 0 0

Employment expenses

17 Business travel and subsistence expenses

£ ⬚ . 0 0

18 Fixed deductions for expenses

£ ⬚ . 0 0

19 Professional fees and subscriptions

£ ⬚ . 0 0

20 Other expenses and capital allowances

£ ⬚ . 0 0

ℹ Share schemes, employment lump sums, compensation, deductions and Seafarers' Earnings Deduction are on the *Additional information* pages enclosed in the tax return pack.

SA102 2014   Page E 1   HMRC 12/13

Task 9(a)

For each statement in connection with capital gains, tick the appropriate box.

	True	False
Payment of capital gains tax is subject to the same rules regarding payments on account as income tax		
The annual exempt amount for capital gains tax is increased for taxpayers born before 6 April 1948		

(b)

A taxpayer had previously bought an asset for £14,000, plus 6% auction commission. He sold it during the tax year for £15,000, having spent £100 to advertise it for sale. The cost of insuring the asset during his ownership was £150.

Calculate the gain or loss using the following computation.

	Amount £
Proceeds	
Total costs	
Gain / Loss	

(c)

Complete the following table to show which statements are true and which are false in connection with capital gains tax.

Statement	True	False
Gifts to charities are exempt from capital gains tax		
Gifts between a father and son are exempt from capital gains tax		
When applying the 5/3 restriction to chattels, the proceeds figure used is before any costs of sale are deducted		
Chattels are defined as tangible moveable property		
Non-wasting chattels are exempt from capital gains tax		

Task 10

Paul bought 18,000 shares in Leicester Ltd for £4.50 per share in October 2000. In April 2012 he took up a rights issue of 4 for 9 at £3 per share. In January 2015, Paul sold 12,000 shares for £6 per share.

Clearly showing the balance of shares, and their value, to carry forward calculate the gain made on these shares. All workings must be shown in your calculations.

Task 11(a)

Emily bought a house on 1 January 2000. She lived in the house until 31 December 2003 when she moved abroad to Dubai to take up a job. She worked there until 30 September 2007, while renting out her own house. She then moved back into her own house from 1 October 2007 until 31 December 2009, when she moved to a new home and put the house on the market. The house was eventually sold on 31 March 2015.

Which periods are treated as occupied and which are not?

Occupation / Deemed Occupation	Non-occupation

(b)

Complete the following sentences.

A taxpayer had capital losses brought forward of £6,000. During the tax year he made two disposals, making a gain of £16,300 on one and a loss of £1,900 on the other.

The amount subject to capital gains tax for the year (after the annual exempt amount) will be

£

The capital loss to be carried forward to be set against future gains will be

£

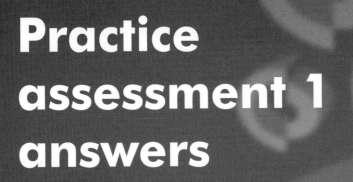

**Practice
assessment 1
answers**

Task 1 (a)

(1)	99 g/km	12%
(2)	140 g/km	21%
(3)	171 g/km	27%
(4)	241 g/km	35%

(b)

(1) The cost of the car used in the benefit in kind computation is **£16,000**

(2) The percentage used in the benefit in kind computation is **26%**

(3) The assessable benefit for Steve relating to the car for 2014/15 is **£1,733**

Task 2 (a)

(1) (b) £75,000

(2) (c) WOULD be treated as being job-related where no accommodation benefit arises; the others would NOT.

(3) (c) £8,325 *(£6,300 + (3.25% x £50,000) + (20% x £2,000))*

(b)

Description	Exempt	Taxable
Interest-free loans not exceeding £10,000	✔	
Cash payment to employee to help with childcare costs		✔
Employer contributions to company pension scheme	✔	
Free meals in a staff restaurant only available to senior managers		✔
Performance related bonus payment		✔
Provision of one mobile telephone and its running costs	✔	
Holiday pay		✔
Use of a bicycle and helmet to commute to work	✔	
Childcare vouchers up to £55 per week for basic rate taxpayers	✔	

Task 3 (a)

	Two bedroom house	One bedroom flat
	£	£
Income	9,400	5,880
Expenses:		
Redecoration	1,510	
Management Charge	1,128	
Council Tax & Rates		1,160
Insurance		370
Wear & tear Allowance		472
Assessable Profit	6,762	3,878

(b)

(1)

	Claiming rent a room relief £	Normal rental income computation £
Income	13,520	13,520
Allowable deductions:		
Rent a room relief	4,250	
Heating		170
Food		1,456
Wear & tear allowance		1,352
Assessable amount	9,270	10,542

(2)   To pay the minimum income tax, Mike should **claim** rent a room relief.

Task 4(a)

Investment	Amount Received £	Assessable Amount £	Tax treated as paid £
Building Society Account	1,500	1,875	375
Dividends from UK Cos.	4,950	5,500	550
Stocks & Shares NISA	190	0	0
Local authority loan interest	1,600	2,000	400
Totals	8,240	9,375	1,325

(b)

Cash NISA limit	£15,000

Task 5

	£
Salary	110,148
Benefit in kind loan	1,160
Entertaining clients	0
Personal pension	0
Bank interest	2,000
Dividend income	3,500
Personal allowance	6,596
Taxable income	110,212

Workings:

Adjusted net income:

£110,148 + £1,160 + £2,000 + £3,500 – (£8,000 x 100/80) = £106,808

Personal allowance:

£10,000 – ((£106,808 – £100,000) x 50%) = £6,596

Task 6(a)

	£
Pension Income	102,000
Bank Interest	750
Sub Total	102,750
Personal Allowance	9,125
Taxable Income	93,625
Tax:	
General (£31,865 + £1,000) x 20%	6,573
(£92,875 – £32,865) x 40%	24,004
Savings £750 x 40%	300
Tax Liability	30,877

Although James is 80 years old his income is too high for him to benefit from the aged allowance. As his adjusted net income is over £100,000 the basic allowance is restricted.

Personal Allowance Working:

Basic Allowance	£10,000
Less ((£102,750 – £1,000) – £100,000) x 50%	£875
	£9,125

(b)

email	
from	Accounting Technician
to	All Staff
subject	Comparison of Tax Implications of Travelling Schemes
date:	XX

You are aware that there is to be a new scheme for business journeys. I want to explain how the tax implications for you compare with the previous scheme.

Under the old scheme you were paid 50p per mile for all business journeys that you undertook in your own car. HMRC rates were lower than this, at 45p per mile for the first 10,000 miles in a tax year, and 25p per mile for any additional miles. This means that up until now you will have paid tax on the difference between the amount that you received and the HMRC rates.

The good news is that under the new pool car scheme there is no tax liability for using the car for business journeys. As you know, the company will also reimburse you for the cost of petrol that you fill up a pool car with, and there will be no tax implications for this either.

Task 7

The income should have been recorded on the self-assessment tax return for 2012/13 that was due to be submitted by 31 January 2014. However changes can be made to a tax return up to one year after that deadline without having to make a formal written application to HMRC. John should therefore make an amendment to his tax return as soon as possible before 31 January 2015.

Assuming that John remains a higher rate taxpayer after this income is disclosed, he will owe 40% x £5,000 = £2,000 additional income tax. This will be subject to interest. There could also be a penalty of up to 30% of the extra tax if the omission is considered 'careless', or up to 70% if the omission was deliberate.

If John chose not to notify HMRC about the omission and it was subsequently discovered by HMRC the penalty could be up to 100% of the additional tax.

Since John is now our client we must encourage him to disclose his omission to HMRC. If he does not do so we will be unable to continue to act for him.

Task 8(a)

	£	£
Income		10,000
Expenditure:		
Council Tax	720	
Water Rates	260	
Insurance	280	
Managing Agent's Charges	800	
Wear & Tear Allowance	902	
		2,962
Assessable Income		7,038

(b) *reproduced opposite*

Property income

Do not include furnished holiday lettings, Real Estate Investment Trust or Property Authorised Investment Funds dividends/distributions here.

20 Total rents and other income from property

£ 1 0 0 0 0 . 0 0

21 Tax taken off any income in box 20 - *read the notes*

£ . 0 0

22 Premiums for the grant of a lease - from box E on the Working Sheet - *read the notes*

£ . 0 0

23 Reverse premiums and inducements

£ . 0 0

Property expenses

24 Rent, rates, insurance, ground rents etc.

£ 1 2 6 0 . 0 0

25 Property repairs and maintenance

£ . 0 0

26 Loan interest and other financial costs

£ . 0 0

27 Legal, management and other professional fees

£ 8 0 0 . 0 0

28 Costs of services provided, including wages

£ . 0 0

29 Other allowable property expenses

£ . 0 0

Calculating your taxable profit or loss

30 Private use adjustment - *read the notes*

£ . 0 0

31 Balancing charges - *read the notes*

£ . 0 0

32 Annual Investment Allowance

£ . 0 0

33 Business Premises Renovation Allowance (Assisted Areas only) - *read the notes*

£ . 0 0

34 All other capital allowances

£ . 0 0

35 Landlord's Energy Saving Allowance

£ . 0 0

36 10% wear and tear allowance - *for furnished residential accommodation only*

£ 9 0 2 . 0 0

37 Rent a Room exempt amount

£ . 0 0

38 Adjusted profit for the year - from box O on the Working Sheet - *read the notes*

£ 7 0 3 8 . 0 0

39 Loss brought forward used against this year's profits

£ . 0 0

40 Taxable profit for the year (box 38 minus box 39)

£ 7 0 3 8 . 0 0

41 Adjusted loss for the year - from box O on the Working Sheet - *read the notes*

£ . 0 0

42 Loss set off against 2013-14 total income - *this will be unusual - read the notes*

£ . 0 0

43 Loss to carry forward to following year, including unused losses brought forward

£ . 0 0

Task 9(a)

	Actual Proceeds Used	Deemed proceeds used	No gain or loss basis
(1) Dave gives an asset to his father		✔	
(2) Peter sells an asset to his friend	✔		
(3) Simon gives an asset to his friend		✔	

(b) **(1)** The gain on the asset is **£11,500**

(2) The amount of loss that will be relieved is **£500**

(3) The capital gains tax payable is **£0**

(4) The loss to be carried forward to the next tax year is **£2,000**

(c)

Asset	Exempt	Chargeable
Land		✔
Principal private residence	✔	
Antique painting valued at £20,000		✔
Unquoted shares		✔
Caravan	✔	
Government securities	✔	
Classic car	✔	
Horse	✔	

Task 10

	Number of Shares	Value £
Purchase	25,000	125,000
Rights	15,000	60,000
Sub total	40,000	185,000
Disposal	10,000	46,250
Balance	30,000	138,750
Proceeds		80,000
Cost		46,250
Gain		33,750

Task 11(a)

Occupation / Deemed Occupation	Non-occupation
1/1/1999 - 31/12/2002	
1/1/2003 - 30/6/2006	
1/7/2006 - 31/12/2010	
1/9/2013 - 1/3/2015	1/1/2011 - 31/8/2013

(b) All the statements are false.

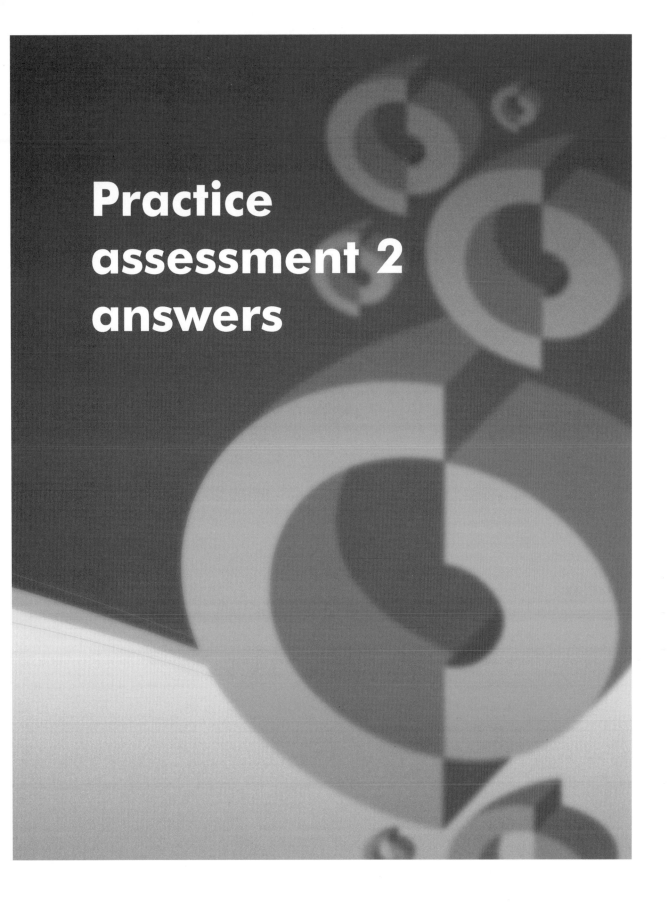

Practice assessment 2 answers

Task 1

Car		%	£
Ford	Scale charge percentage	20	
	Taxable benefit on provision of the car		2,375
	Taxable benefit on provision of fuel		1,808
Kia	Scale charge percentage	20	
	Taxable benefit on provision of the car		3,103
	Taxable benefit on provision of fuel		2,531
Total taxable benefit			9,817

Task 2

(a) ONLY **Subscription to gym that is also used by non-employees** will result in an assessable benefit in kind; the other options will NOT.

(b)

	Assessable amount £
Use of computer games console	70
Interest free loan	357
Mileage allowance	2,550

Task 3(a)

	£
Income	6,600
Expenditure:	
Resurfacing path	200
Building and contents insurance	342
Irrecoverable rent insurance	120
Agent's management charges	792
Repairs to central heating	250
Wear and tear	660
PROFIT	4,236

(b)

	2012/13	2013/14	2014/15
	£	£	£
Loss relieved	0	2,800	4,300
Total assessable property income	7,900	200	12,950

Task 4

Income	Amount received	Assessable amount	Tax deducted at source	Additional tax payable
	£	£	£	£
Interest from NISA	1,400	0.00	0.00	0.00
Interest from Bank	5,500	6,875	1,375.00	2.00
Dividends	1,800	2,000	200.00	450.00

Task 5

	£
Basic salary	94,500
Bonus	4,000
Benefit in kind accommodation	6,455
Benefit in kind entertaining	0
Employer's pension contribution	0
Employee's pension contribution	4,725
Gift aid payment	0
Dividend income	3,500
Personal allowance	9,135
Taxable income	94,595

Workings:

Adjusted net income:

£94,500 + £4,000 + £6,455 − £4,725 + £3,500 − (£1,600 x 100/80) = £101,730

Personal allowance:

£10,000 − ((£101,730 − £100,000) x 0.5) = £9,135

Task 6(a)

	Workings	£
Employment income		32,000
Property income		10,100
Building society interest	£3,300 x 100/80	4,125
Dividends	£3,690 x 100 / 90	4,100
		50,325
Personal allowance		10,000
Taxable income		40,325
General income	42,100 – 10,000 = 32,100	
	31,865 x 20%	6,373
	235 x 40%	94
Savings income	4,125 x 40%	1,650
Dividend income	4,100 x 32.5%	1,332
Total tax liability		9,449

(b)

If the payments are made under the gift aid scheme, then the amount paid (£1,200 per year in your case) will be treated as net of tax, ie 80% of the donation, and the charity could reclaim the £300 tax deducted, the remaining 20%, from HMRC.

Because you are a higher rate taxpayer there is also a tax advantage for you. The gross amount (£1,200 x 100/80 = £1,500) will be used to increase the basic rate band. Using your 2014/15 figures as an example, the band would increase from £31,865 to £33,365 and you would therefore save (40% – 20% = 20%) tax on some of your general and savings income. This would reduce your tax liability by £300.

There are therefore benefits for both you and the charity from using the gift aid scheme.

Task 7

There will be a penalty due on the late payment of the balancing payment for 2013/14. This will be 5% of the amount of £5,100 as it is late by more than 30 days (£255). As it is not more than 6 months late a further penalty of 5% is avoided. There is no penalty due on the payment on account of £9,300.

Interest is, however, due on both the balancing payment and the payment on account. This will be at an annual percentage (currently 3%), and will be applied to the full amount of £14,400 for four months. This interest will amount to approximately £144.

Task 8

HM Revenue & Customs

Employment
Tax year 6 April 2013 to 5 April 2014

Your name

Your Unique Taxpayer Reference (UTR)

Complete an *Employment* page for each employment or directorship

1 Pay from this employment – the total from your P45 or P60 - *before tax was taken off*

£ 2 8 3 5 0 · 0 0

2 UK tax taken off pay in box 1

£ — · 0 0

3 Tips and other payments not on your P60 - *read the Employment notes*

£ · 0 0

4 PAYE tax reference of your employer (on your P45/P60)

/

5 Your employer's name

6 If you were a company director, put 'X' in the box

7 And, if the company was a close company, put 'X' in the box

8 If you are a part-time teacher in England or Wales and are on the Repayment of Teachers' Loans Scheme for this employment, put 'X' in the box

Benefits from your employment – use your form P11D (or equivalent information)

9 Company cars and vans - *the total 'cash equivalent' amount*

£ 4 6 5 0 · 0 0

10 Fuel for company cars and vans - *the total 'cash equivalent' amount*

£ 6 9 0 0 · 0 0

11 Private medical and dental insurance - *the total 'cash equivalent' amount*

£ · 0 0

12 Vouchers, credit cards and excess mileage allowance

£ · 0 0

13 Goods and other assets provided by your employer - *the total value or amount*

£ · 0 0

14 Accommodation provided by your employer - *the total value or amount*

£ · 0 0

15 Other benefits (including interest-free and low interest loans) - *the total 'cash equivalent' amount*

£ 3 5 0 · 0 0

16 Expenses payments received and balancing charges

£ 7 8 0 · 0 0

Employment expenses

17 Business travel and subsistence expenses

£ 7 8 0 · 0 0

18 Fixed deductions for expenses

£ · 0 0

19 Professional fees and subscriptions

£ 2 0 0 · 0 0

20 Other expenses and capital allowances

£ · 0 0

Task 9(a)

	True	False
A chattel bought and sold for less than £6,000 is exempt from capital gains tax	✔	
Transfers between spouses are carried out on a 'no gain, no loss' basis	✔	
Capital gains tax will be incurred on the increase in value of investments between the date of purchase and the date of the owners' death		✔
Mechanical chattels (for example clocks) owned for personal use are exempt from capital gains tax	✔	

(b)   Loss of £1,000

(c)

	£
Proceeds or deemed proceeds	11,000
Cost or deemed cost	9,400
Gain or loss	1,600

Task 10

		Number of shares	Value £
April 2003	Purchase	800	3,000
May 2009	Purchase	1,200	4,680
December 2010	Rights issue	400	800
		2,400	8,480
November 2014	Disposal	500	1,767
	Balance	1,900	6,713
December 2014	Purchase	100	630
	Balance	2,000	7,343
		£	
	Proceeds	3,000	
	Cost	1,767	
	Gain	1,233	

Task 11(a)

Total period of ownership in months	126
Period of actual occupation in months	36
Period of deemed occupation in months	18
Chargeable gain on the sale of the house	£41,714

Gain Working: (£198,000 − £125,000) x 72/126 = £41,714

(b)

	Capital Loss 2013/14 £	Capital Loss 2014/15 £	Capital Gain 2014/15 £	Amount of Loss to be relieved 2014/15 £	Amount of Loss carried forward £
Brian	6,900	4,500	15,000	4,500	6,900
Colin	0	6,900	15,000	6,900	0
Denise	6,900	0	15,000	4,000	2,900

Practice assessment 3 answers

Task 1

Car	Percentage applicable based on CO₂ emissions %	Cost of car used in benefit calculation £	Benefit in kind £
Jaguar	23	52,000	2,990
Range Rover	35	73,200	19,215
Total			22,205

Task 2

(a) ONLY **Petrol for travel from home to work in a company car** will result in an assessable benefit in kind; the other options will NOT.

(b)

	Benefit £
On 6 April an employee was provided with an interest free loan of £15,000. During the tax year he made three repayments, each of £2,000. The remainder of the loan was still outstanding at the end of the tax year.	390
On 6 April an employee was allowed the use of a home cinema system that had previously been used by the company. The home cinema had originally cost the company £1,500, but its market value on 6 April was £1,000.	200

(c)

Description	Exempt	Taxable
Provision of a chauffeur for business and private journeys		✔
Long service award in cash for employee with 10 year's service		✔
Counselling services	✔	
Free meals in a staff restaurant available to all staff	✔	
Provision of free UK health insurance		✔

(d)

Business mileage and rate paid	Increase tax liability	Reduce tax liability
5,000 miles at 50p per mile	✔	
15,000 miles at 45p per mile	✔	
15,000 miles at 38p per mile		✔
20,000 miles at 25p per mile		✔

Task 3(a)

	Allowable deduction	Not an allowable deduction
Depreciation of property		✔
Monthly repayment of mortgage capital		✔
Advertising for tenants	✔	
Repainting windows	✔	
Insurance against irrecoverable rent	✔	
Installing central heating		✔
Capital allowances related to holiday lettings	✔	

(b)

	True	False
If a taxpayer is claiming rent a room relief he cannot claim any other deductions from the rental income	✔	
The time limit to claim rent a room relief is one year after the due date for the online tax return	✔	

(c)

Statement	
Yes, this qualifies	
No, this doesn't qualify only because it was not actually let for long enough	
No, this doesn't qualify only because it wasn't available for letting for long enough	✔
No, this doesn't qualify because it was neither available nor actually let for long enough	

Task 4(a)

Investment	Amount Received	Assessable Amount	Tax treated as paid
	£	£	£
Bank deposit account	1,600	2,000	400
Cash NISA	270	0	0
Government stocks (gilts)	1,200	1,200	0
Totals	3,070	3,200	400

(b)

	Assessable amount	Total tax liability
	£	£
Dividends received of £3,600	4,000	1,500

Task 5

	£
Pension	19,650
NISA interest	0
Bank interest	4,000
Dividend income	5,500
Gift aid payments	0
Total income	29,150
Personal allowance	10,275
Taxable income	18,875

Workings:

Adjusted net income:

£19,650 + £4,000 + £5,500 − (£1,360 x 100/80) = £27,450

Personal allowance:

£10,500 − ((£27,450 − £27,000) x 50%) = £10,275

Task 6(a)

		£
Employment Income		127,500
Dividends		1,000
		128,500
Personal Allowance	(See below)	5,750
Taxable		122,750
Tax on general income:		
(£31,865 + £20,000)	£51,865 at 20%	10,373
(£127,500 − £5,750 − £51,865)	£69,885 at 40%	27,954
Tax on dividends	£1,000 at 32.5%	325
Tax liability		38,652
Workings:	Basic Personal Allowance	10,000
Less	50% (£128,500 − £20,000 − £100,000)	4,250
		5,750

6(b) is on the next page

Task 6(b)

---

email

from: Accounting Technician

to: All staff

subject: Payroll Giving Scheme

date: XX/XX/XXXX

I am writing to explain the payroll giving scheme that the company is now operating.

The scheme is entirely voluntary, but any member of staff may use it to make regular donations to a charity of their choice. The payroll department will arrange to deduct a regular amount that you choose from your income before income tax is calculated on the balance. This will give you full tax relief from any donations, so for example a payment of £50 per month would only actually cost you £40 per month if you are a basic rate (20%) taxpayer. If you were paying tax at higher than the basic rate the cost to you of the same donation would be even less.

This scheme provides the same level of tax relief as the gift aid scheme that you may have heard of. Gift aid does not operate through the payroll, but allows individuals to make one-off or regular donations to charity net of a 20% tax deduction. This means that a donation by a basic rate taxpayer of £50 would again only cost £40. Higher rate taxpayers would receive additional tax relief through an increase in the basic rate band by the gross amount of the donation, so less tax is paid at the higher rate.

You can use either or both schemes if you wish to donate to charity.

Task 7

Explanation of amounts payable

On 31 January 2016 the final payment for 2014/15 will be due for both income tax and capital gains tax. This will be calculated as:

Income tax for 2014/15	£26,800
Less already paid on account (2 x £11,625)	£23,250
	£3,550
Capital gains tax for 2014/15	£10,250
Total tax relating to 2014/15	£13,800

In addition a payment on account for 2015/16 will be due at the same time. This is based on 50% of the total income tax for 2014/15 of £26,800 – i.e £13,400. There is no payment on account relating to capital gains tax.

The total payable on 31 January 2016 will therefore be:

Total tax relating to 2014/15	£13,800
First payment on account for 2015/16	£13,400
	£27,200

A second payment on account for 2015/16 of £13,400 will be due on 31 July 2016.

Implications of not making payments when due

Interest will be due on all late payments. The interest rate is currently 3% pa.

In addition, penalties are payable for late payment of the balancing payment for a tax year (not on payments on account). If a balancing payment is between 30 days and 6 months late the penalty would be 5% of the tax.

In this case it would therefore be 5% x £13,800 = £690.

If the payment was over 6 months late there would be a further 5% penalty, and another 5% if over 12 months late.

Task 8

<table>
<tr><td colspan="2">HM Revenue & Customs</td><td colspan="2" align="right">Employment
Tax year 6 April 2013 to 5 April 2014</td></tr>
</table>

Your name

J A C K   P R I C E

Your Unique Taxpayer Reference (UTR)

Complete an *Employment* page for each employment or directorship

1 Pay from this employment – the total from your P45 or P60 – *before tax was taken off*

£ 4 4 6 0 0 . 0 0

2 UK tax taken off pay in box 1

£ – 9 1 0 0 . 0 0

3 Tips and other payments not on your P60
- *read the Employment notes*

£ . 0 0

4 PAYE tax reference of your employer (on your P45/P60)

      /

5 Your employer's name

P P P   L I M I T E D

6 If you were a company director, put 'X' in the box

7 And, if the company was a close company, put 'X' in the box

8 If you are a part-time teacher in England or Wales and are on the Repayment of Teachers' Loans Scheme for this employment, put 'X' in the box

Benefits from your employment – use your form P11D (or equivalent information)

9 Company cars and vans
- *the total 'cash equivalent' amount*

£ 3 0 0 0 . 0 0

10 Fuel for company cars and vans
- *the total 'cash equivalent' amount*

£ 3 0 3 0 . 0 0

11 Private medical and dental insurance
- *the total 'cash equivalent' amount*

£ . 0 0

12 Vouchers, credit cards and excess mileage allowance

£ . 0 0

13 Goods and other assets provided by your employer
- *the total value or amount*

£ . 0 0

14 Accommodation provided by your employer
- *the total value or amount*

£ . 0 0

15 Other benefits (including interest-free and low interest loans) - *the total 'cash equivalent' amount*

£ . 0 0

16 Expenses payments received and balancing charges

£ 3 8 0 . 0 0

Employment expenses

17 Business travel and subsistence expenses

£ 3 8 0 . 0 0

18 Fixed deductions for expenses

£ . 0 0

19 Professional fees and subscriptions

£ . 0 0

20 Other expenses and capital allowances

£ . 0 0

Task 9(a)

	True	False
Payment of capital gains tax is subject to the same rules regarding payments on account as income tax		✔
The annual exempt amount for capital gains tax is increased for taxpayers born before 6 April 1948		✔

(b)

	Amount £
Proceeds	15,000
Total costs	14,940
Gain	60

(c)

Statement	True	False
Gifts to charities are exempt from capital gains tax	✔	
Gifts between a father and son are exempt from capital gains tax		✔
When applying the 5/3 restriction to chattels, the proceeds figure used is before any costs of sale are deducted	✔	
Chattels are defined as tangible moveable property	✔	
Non-wasting chattels are exempt from capital gains tax		✔

Task 10

October 2000	18,000	£81,000
April 2012	8,000	£24,000
	26,000	£105,000
Disposal	12,000	£48,462
Pool balance	14,000	£56,538
Proceeds		£72,000
Cost		£48,462
Gain		£23,538

Task 11(a)

Occupation / Deemed Occupation	Non-occupation
1 Jan 2000 - 31 Dec 2003 1 Jan 2004 - 30 Sept 2007 1 Oct 2007 - 31 Dec 2009 1 Oct 2013 - 31 March 2015	1 Jan 2010 - 30 Sept 2013

(b)

The amount subject to capital gains tax for the year (after the annual exempt amount) will be **£0.**

The capital loss to be carried forward to be set against future gains will be **£2,600.**

for your notes

for your notes

for your notes

for your notes

for your notes